Table of Contents

I0484720

Acronyms and Abbreviations

AACSB	Association to Advance Collegiate Schools of Business
AfDB	African Development Bank
AmCham	American Chamber of Commerce
ANDE	Aspen Network of Development Entrepreneurs
AUC	American University in Cairo
BGI	Business Growth Initiative
BoP	Base of the Pyramid
CEED	Center for Entrepreneurship and Executive Development
CEO	Chief Executive Officer
CID	[Harvard] Center for International Development
CRDF	Civilian Research and Development Foundation
CSTS	[Santa Clara University's] Center for Science, Technology and Society
DCA	Development Credit Authority
EDC	Education Development Center
EDP	Entrepreneurship Development Program
EFE	Education for Employment
EFL	Entrepreneurial Finance Lab
EGAT	Economic Growth and Trade
EIP	Entrepreneurship and Innovation Program
EO	Entrepreneur's Organization
GBF	Grassroots Business Fund
GBSN	Global Business School Network
GDA	Global Development Alliance
GDP	Gross Domestic Product
GEP	Global Entrepreneurship Program
GEPI	Global Entrepreneurship Program Indonesia
GER	Growing Entrepreneurship Rapidly
GEM	Global Entrepreneurship Monitor
GEW	Global Entrepreneurship Week
GITP	Global Technology Innovation Partners
GSBI	Global Social Benefit Incubator
GSEA	Global Student Entrepreneur Awards
ICT	Information and Communication Technology
IFC	International Finance Corporation
IT	Information Technology
ITIDA	Information Technology Industry Development Agency
MBA	Master of Business Administration
MENA	Middle East and North Africa
MIT	Massachusetts Institute of Technology
MMC	Muslim-Majority Country
NGO	Non-Governmental Organization
NYU	New York University
PEC	Personal Entrepreneurial Competencies
PPP	Public-Private Partnership
SEAF	Small Enterprise Assistance Fund
SME	Small-to-Medium Enterprises
UAE	United Arab Emirates
UN	United Nations
USAID	United States Agency for International Development
USG	United States Government

Acknowledgements

The Business Growth Initiative (BGI) team comprised of Weidemann Associates, J.E. Austin Associates and Management Systems International (MSI), would like to sincerely thank USAID not only for sponsoring the creation of this toolkit, but also for their hard work and guidance throughout its development. In particular, we would like to acknowledge Kathleen Wu, BGI's COTR, for her thoughtful leadership throughout this process, and Kristin O'Planick who provided valuable technical input during its writing.

We would also like to thank the U.S. Department of State's Global Entrepreneurship Program (GEP) staff; Lorraine Hariton, Steven Koltai, Cleveland Charles, Anne Park, Brenda Rios and Samantha Toth; for their time and dedication to this project. All of them are true champions for entrepreneurship and work every day to promote GEP's mission and goals. We hope this toolkit provides practical recommendations they can use to strengthen what is already the foundation for an important component of the Department of State's overall objectives.

The BGI team also wishes to thank the GEP partners who through interviews, meetings, phone calls, and numerous emails helped us develop our list of recommendations and best practices. Each graciously provided time and insight for improving GEP, as well as designing, implementing and monitoring entrepreneurship programs in countries throughout the world. The BGI team took significant efforts to ensure feedback and recommendations provided by those interviewed were accurately captured and reflected in this toolkit.

Lastly, we would like to thank our colleagues, Marialyce Mutchler, BGI Project Director, and Martin Webber, Jarrett Creasy, Melissa Brinkerhoff, and Megan Delph, for providing technical inputs, logistical help, and overall support to create this toolkit.

A Note to Our Audience:
How to Read and Use the *Entrepreneurship Toolkit*

The *Entrepreneurship Toolkit* has been developed to help USAID Mission and U.S. Embassy officers in the field in the design, implementation, and monitoring of entrepreneurship development programs. The Business Growth Initiative (BGI) project, throughout the course of interviewing Global Entrepreneurship Program (GEP) partners and non-GEP organizations, and supplemented by external research, actively focused on identifying, categorizing and compiling real-life examples that can be accurately defined as best practices of entrepreneurship, defined as a method or technique that has consistently shown results superior to those achieved with other means.

While it was certainly not BGI's intention, nor within its scope, to develop a comprehensive guide to showcase all potential entrepreneurship best practices, significant efforts were made to find unique and compelling examples that can be effectively used by USG officials. With this in mind, BGI looked for a whole host of different approaches that have been successfully used, in order to provide its' audience with a fair and representative sample of the types of activities implemented in the field of entrepreneurship.

The BGI team examined entrepreneurship by utilizing the six pillar framework developed by GEP below:

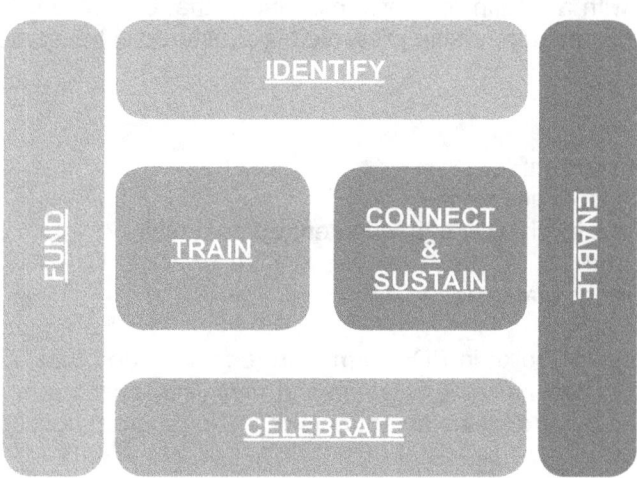

The decision to adopt GEP's approach was taken to continue to leverage the progress it has made in effectively promoting entrepreneurship and to ensure GEP's partner contributions are clearly recognized. Furthermore, it provides readers a holistic overview of the topic, and the opportunity to learn about each critical component inherent in an entrepreneurship program:

• *Identify:* Identifying entrepreneurs is the first step to enabling them to succeed. The ability to consistently develop a pool of potential and existing entrepreneurs requires innovative strategic actions and is integral in building the foundation of a strong entrepreneurial ecosystem.

• *Train:* Many entrepreneurs do not have access to educational opportunities that allow them to gain the skills and knowledge they need to succeed in opening and operating a business. To rectify this deficiency, it is crucial to establish a framework of training that fosters knowledge transfer and capacity building.

• *Connect & Sustain:* The ability and need to build relationships between entrepreneurs and mentors is increasing as globalization and its effects continue to expand. Burgeoning entrepreneurs can gain invaluable assistance from veteran business leaders to help them continue developing their acumen to successfully lead their organizations.

- *Fund:* The lifeblood of any successful organization is a consistent flow of revenue to drive operations. Entrepreneurs must often operate in an arena that provides little opportunity to secure required capital. In light of this, it is important to link entrepreneurs with a variety of investors to ensure they have the financial means necessary to establish and build upon business ideas.

- *Enable:* Entrepreneurs are directly affected by the economic, legal, and cultural elements of the business environment within which they operate. As such, efforts must continually be made to establish a facilitative, rather than combative, economic framework to improve the likelihood of entrepreneurs' success.

- *Celebrate:* Increased visibility of successful entrepreneurs builds enhanced awareness of their positive role in society and encourages a multiplier effect to occur, resulting in more people becoming interested and engaged in entrepreneurial activity themselves.

BGI also developed a seventh category titled "Mixed Models" for those organizations that are primarily operating in more than one of the aforementioned components. For example, Oasis 500 is a multi-faceted organization that is actively involved in training, connecting, sustaining and funding entrepreneurs. The Queen Rania Center for Entrepreneurship, which provides both training and focuses on the celebration of entrepreneurs, also appears within this category.

This toolkit provides readers with a wealth of useful information that can be easily used to guide strategic decision making. Each pillar of entrepreneurship presented is structured in the same way and includes:

- Best practices;
- Case studies;
- Key questions for program design;
- Lessons learned for future USG assistance;
- Contact information for firms involved in promoting entrepreneurship;
- Links to USAID projects; and
- Links to publications/reference materials.

When using the Entrepreneurship Toolkit in PDF form, it is recommended that USG officers select "Read Mode" from the <View> menu to best navigate between and within sections. Furthermore, they should follow the four-step process outline below to develop an entrepreneurship program best suited to their needs.

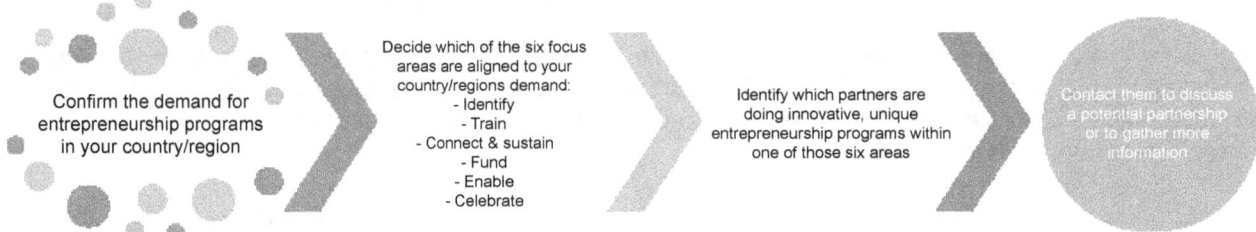

By doing so, officers will be able to formulate needed answers to key questions about establishment of an entrepreneurship program:

- Why is assistance to entrepreneurs needed?
- What type of entrepreneurs will the program focus on helping?
- Which of the six entrepreneurship components is most needed?
- What organizations may be available to help?
- What prior experience could the USG leverage?
- What additional resources and materials are available to reference?

Importance and Role of Entrepreneurship in Developing Countries

What is entrepreneurship?

Although several different concepts and definitions of entrepreneurship exist, one commonly used definition is: "the capacity and willingness to undertake conception, organization, and management of a productive venture with all attendant risks, while seeking profit as a reward.[1]

Entrepreneurship is widely regarded as critical for economic development; however the topic does not play an explicit part in the most influential models of economic growth or development assistance programs. Entrepreneurship is hard to measure. The most ambitious empirical research effort is the Global Entrepreneurship Monitor (GEM), a 12-year-old program that attempts to measure the level of entrepreneurial activity in a large number of countries. The latest (2010) GEM report, covering 59 countries, defines an entrepreneur as someone who started a new business during the year or who ran a business that was less than 3 ½ years old and was still economically viable. The survey identified approximately 110 million people who started businesses in the countries surveyed during 2010 and another 140 million people between the ages of 18 and 64 who were continuing to operate businesses they had started less than 3 ½ years earlier.[2]

Entrepreneurial activity is not always a response to business opportunity. Some analysts distinguish between "opportunity entrepreneurship" and "necessity entrepreneurship". In settings where labor supply greatly exceeds the number of paid jobs available, people often start micro and small businesses primarily because few other income-earning opportunities are available to them. They thus become entrepreneurs not by choice, but by necessity. A key difference to recognize is that businesses started by opportunity entrepreneurs have the potential to grow and hire additional labor, while enterprises created out of necessity by entrepreneurs are very unlikely to do so. The focus of this toolkit is centered on opportunity entrepreneurship.

Entrepreneurship is sometimes measured using the numbers of people who are self-employed; however, this can be misleading when a large number of self-employed people are entrepreneurs out of necessity rather than opportunity. In any case, the number of entrepreneurs in a country is only a rough measure of the power of its entrepreneurial ecosystem. The quality of its entrepreneurs is also important, and even harder to measure.

An Entrepreneur, Sure. But what type?

Need-based entrepreneurs are those who start micro or small businesses out of necessity to maintain their livelihood. Traditionally, these are informal, family owned business selling small hand-made items or food near their homes; they often do not hire other employees.

High-growth entrepreneurs are those who traditionally formalize their businesses, do so out of opportunity, and often earn income, hire employees, and over time contribute to a sector's growth by introducing a new product into the market.

What is the relationship between entrepreneurship and economic development?

Economic development may be defined as sustained improvement in the economic well-being of the population. This definition incorporates economic growth (commonly measured by increases in GDP per capita), but also involves significant changes in the structure of the economy. These changes gradually shift the focus of national production from agriculture and other primary activities to manufacturing and eventually to services. In the process of this structural re-alignment, modern technologies are increasingly used. Bringing about structural or systemic changes in the economy that can be critical for economic development is largely the job of entrepreneurs.

---

[1] http://www.businessdictionary.com/definition/entrepreneurship.html
[2] Global Entrepreneurship Monitor 2010 Global Report

Entrepreneurship fosters economic development by raising income and increasing the number of well-paid jobs available. In low-income economies, most members of the labor force are self-employed persons or unpaid family workers who work in agriculture or in very small scale industrial or service establishments. The relative importance of these forms of employment declines as economic development proceeds. It is therefore the creation of more paid employment that is directly linked to structural, economic improvement. As Adam Smith emphasized more than three centuries ago, economic development involves broadening markets and increasing division of labor.

Nations develop through a combination of successful entrepreneurship and the force of established corporations. However, the mixture varies at different levels of GDP per capita. At low levels of national income, self-employment provides jobs and markets. However, as GDP per capita rises, the adoption of new technologies and growing economies of scale allow larger firms to satisfy the increasing demand of growing markets and to increase their role in the economy. Rising income levels create business opportunities and allow more individuals the resources necessary to utilize them. In low-income countries, inefficient markets create opportunities that can be seized upon by alert entrepreneurs; in richer and more dynamic economies, more creative innovation will be required.

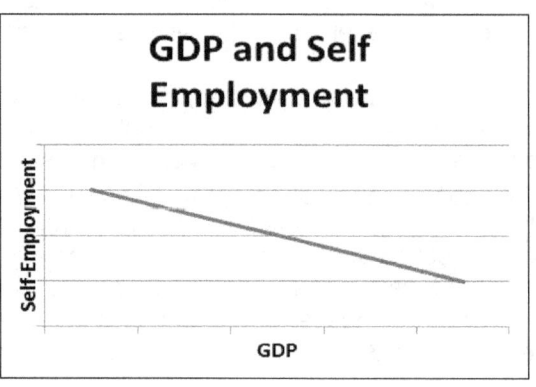

Innovation, that is, the adoption of new technologies, is an important entrepreneurial function, which in developed countries usually involves the application of basic science and engineering to create entirely new products and processes. In developing countries, transfering existing technologies from more developed countries and adapting them to suit local markets and conditions is likely to be involved.

Quality not Quantity

In efforts to promote entrepreneurship that ultimately stimulates broad-based economic growth, particular attention should be paid to the quality of entrepreneur, meaning, those that might end up hiring large numbers of people, introduce a new product or service into a sector, or generate substantial revenue such that incomes will raise and business flow will increase, and thus positively impact the economy.

The development of entrepreneurship has great potential for benefiting the broader society, as well as, the individual entrepreneur. It can stimulate job creation and thereby provide increased incomes and improved welfare to members of society who have little to sell beyond their own labor. Because of these external benefits, a case exists for government and donor support. This support should focus not only on quantity, as in the number of entrepreneurs, but also quality, in terms of the type of impact they generate for society (e.g., "high-impact" entrepreneurs).

Can entrepreneurship be promoted?

The ability and extent to which entrepreneurship can be promoted, by actors in both the public and private sectors, is an issue that is significantly debated among experts in the field. One view, supported by those who favor a lone macroeconomic development approach, is that the role of government is realistically limited to establishing an appropriate institutional framework. In practical terms, this translates to creating a welcoming environment for business, including such matters as property rights, contract enforcement, good infrastructure, and diminishing burdensome regulations, taxation, and corruption. While these matters are certainly important, a complementary view is that a variety of interventions, including the role of academia and training institutions, can and should be used to spur entrepreneurial development.

What are the best ways of promoting entrepreneurship?

While use of the six pillars of entrepreneurship drives project or program formulation, individuals should also evaluate the economic framework that entrepreneurs must work within, as well as gauge the level of entrepreneurial spirit that exists within their respective country. One useful framework suggests that entrepreneurship will develop if three key conditions are present.[3] First, there must be *opportunity* for new enterprises to exist and for entrepreneurs to succeed through their own efforts. Second, there must be a *propensity to enterprise*, involving such characteristics as an urge for

Three Conditions Necessary for Entrepreneurship to Flourish

1. *Opportunity,* for new enterprises to enter the market
2. *Propensity to enterprise,* willingness to bear risk and a desire to be independent
3. *Ability to enterprise,* technical and business capabilities to start and manage a business

excellence, a willingness to bear risk, and a desire to be independent. Third, the *ability to enterprise* must be present; meaning the technical and business capabilities required to start and manage a business must exist.

Developing country governments, NGOs, business associations, and international development agencies have collectively undertaken hundreds of entrepreneurship development programs over the years, working in all three of these areas.

Various efforts have been made to improve *entrepreneurial opportunity.* One important set of policies addresses the effect of start-up costs and business regulation on enterprise creation. Entrepreneurs are clearly constrained by the regulatory cost, not only of starting, but also of operating and sometimes closing a business. The policy implication is that these costs should be reduced and the regulations should be simplified. The World Bank's Doing Business reports have shown that these costs can be high in terms of money and time. Many developing countries, including some Muslim-majority countries (MMCs),[4] rank low among the nations of the world in terms of the ease of doing business in general, as well as in specific aspects of business regulation, such as starting a new enterprise.

In countries with highly distorted institutional and policy frameworks, entrepreneurial energy may be diverted from producing true economic value to avoiding burdensome taxes and regulations, and even into destructive activities- such as the drug trade. Predatory actions on the part of those with political and military power can also inhibit tntrepreneurship. Barriers to entrepreneurial activities are often harsh and diverse in fragile states and conflict-affected environments.

Some of the most important measures for improving productive entrepreneurship concern improvements in a country's institutional framework. An appropriate framework includes secure property rights, the rule of law, a reasonable level of taxation on profits, currency convertibility, contract enforcement, financial stability, control of monopolies, and sound employment practices; additionally, such a framework ensures that productive entrepreneurs can capture the profits and other rewards of their activities.

Another approach to increasing entrepreneurial opportunity is to raise the non-pecuniary benefits of entrepreneurship by improving the entrepreneur's social position. A culture that is less critical of inequality, business failure, and personal independence may be more conducive to entrepreneurship. One way to help bring about such change is to promote the image of successful entrepreneurs as role models. Furthermore, efforts to promote the tangible benefits of entrepreneurship, such as increased job creation, are important in creating a more positive image of the field itself. It would be difficult, in terms of both time and money required, however, for governments and other development actors to significantly change cultural norms.

---

[3] Based on Devi R. Gnyawali and Daniel S. Fogel, "Environments for Entrepreneurship Development: Key Dimensions and Research Implications," *Entrepreneurship: Theory and Practice* 18 (Summer): 43-62.

[4] The lowest-ranked Muslim-majority countries are Afghanistan, Iraq, Mauritania, Sudan, Uzbekistan, Syria, Tajikistan, Algeria, West Bank and Gaza, Iran, and Indonesia. By contrast, Saudi Arabia, Malaysia, the United Arab Emirates, Kyrgyzstan, and Qatar are among the 50 easiest countries in which to do business according to the latest rankings.

Entrepreneurship in many regions of the world can be strengthened through a multi-pronged strategy that promotes the rule of law and strengthens the private sector, as well as civil society in general.[5] Educating the public about the importance of pro-business reforms could help build a consensus and improve a country's or region's economic standing.

Psychology-based projects that aim to build up *entrepreneurial propensities* are one example of an attempt to analyze and understand entrepreneurial behavior and actions (see example 1).

Example 1: EMPRETEC and the Behavioral Approach

EMPRETEC is a UN-funded entrepreneurship training program, based on USAID-funded research, undertaken by Management Systems International and McBer and Company. It has been implemented as the Entrepreneurship Development Program (EDP) by Management Systems International in about 40 countries.

The underlying principle of EMPRETEC is that entrepreneurship is a set of behaviors and practices that can be observed and acquired. The behavioral approach to entrepreneurship suggests that the proclivity and facility with which an individual manifests these behaviors can be significantly strengthened in individuals by appropriate exposure and training. Equally important, the behavioral approach suggests that entrepreneurial acumen can be meaningfully and accurately assessed by measuring the extent to which an individual demonstrates key entrepreneurial behaviors.

In an effort to identify these behaviors, a 5-year, $1 million dollar USAID-funded research project analyzed the actions and thought processes of successful entrepreneurs in several countries and isolated the behaviors distinguishing these individuals from less successful entrepreneurs in their own countries. Among the findings of this research was the fact that these behaviors were remarkably consistent from country to country. The research and subsequent testing identified ten Personal Entrepreneurial Competencies (PECs) and 30 behavioral indicators found to be most useful for detecting and strengthening entrepreneurial potential.

Many different projects have focused on micro, small, and medium enterprises and attempted to improve *entrepreneurial ability* in various ways. Their activities include: facilitating the provision of seed capital and enterprise finance; creating business services and supporting infrastructure; developing business networks and clusters; offering work experience through apprenticeship programs; providing entrepreneurial and managerial training; supplying skill training (both on and off the job); promoting basic education; and strengthening the position of women and youth in business (see example 2).

Example 2: The Women's Entrepreneurship and Skills Development for Food Security Pilot Project

This African Development Bank (AfDB) project is training 4,500 women in basic business management and agro-processing skills in an effort to introduce agro-processing and trading as a means of livelihood for rural agriculture-dependent households. Furthermore, it aims to train 900 women in advanced entrepreneurship and business start-up skills.

Basic business management training is delivered in 350 group training sessions on functional literary, basic business management, rural marketing, fundamental bookkeeping, human resource management, and leadership and communication skills.

The women from the second group of trainees are expected to become full-time entrepreneurs and business owners. The training they receive includes business start-up strategies, registration, product development, market surveying, and guidance to accessing working capital.

---

[5] See Kuran.

What has been the experience with efforts to promote entrepreneurship?

Designing policies for the promotion of entrepreneurship is complicated.[6] The benefits of simplifying business regulation, especially entry conditions, as an effective policy for fostering entrepreneurial activity are relatively well established. There is also some reason to expect benefits from entrepreneurial education. A review in the late 1990s indicated that entrepreneurship can be taught, or at least encouraged, through entrepreneurship education.[7] In general, however, solid evidence on the effectiveness of the many approaches taken to promoting entrepreneurship over the years is hard to find.

With this being said, the United States Agency for International Development (USAID) has been a leading provider of entrepreneurship development worldwide for decades. Research conducted by BGI discovered more than 100 projects that have been implemented in 52 countries since the 1990s. It is important to note that USAID has typically not designed and implemented stand-alone entrepreneurship programs, but instead has woven elements of entrepreneurship into the most notable enterprise development projects (see USAID Project Summary). USAID also maintains a website (http://egateg.usaid.gov/) which showcases several of its projects geared towards entrepreneurship development, including: an effort to strengthen entrepreneurship in Mongolia (see example 3); an ICT entrepreneurship program in Egypt; an entrepreneurship education project in Lebanon; training for current and aspiring entrepreneurs in Kyrgyzstan; a center for entrepreneurship training in Cambodia; a center for entrepreneurship and executive development in Bulgaria (see example 4); and a Junior Achievement enterprise education program in Albania. While these efforts have begun to yield gains towards fostering entrepreneurship on a global basis, they need to be continued through implementation of a more intentional, concentrated approach to reach a "tipping point," when pro-entrepreneurship actions are implemented and recognized consistently.

Example 3: The Growing Entrepreneurship Rapidly (GER) Initiative

The USAID-funded Growing Entrepreneurship Rapidly (GER) Initiative supports local entrepreneurship and facilitates employment in Mongolia's peri-urban areas. The program operates twenty business and employment centers serving clients in small manufacturing (e.g., wood, metal-working, and textiles), construction, agribusiness and trade services. These centers provide services such as group development, consulting, training, loan facilitation, employment matching, business-to-business input and sales linkages, as well as business, market and legal information.

Example 4: Center for Entrepreneurship and Executive Development (CEED)

The Center for Entrepreneurship and Executive Development (CEED) is a USAID-developed and funded initiative, utilizing reflows from the Small Enterprise Assistance Fund's (SEAF) various venture capital investment funds, to provide entrepreneurs and their respective executive teams with the knowledge, skills, and business networks needed to accelerate their businesses. CEED has active centers operating in Slovenia, Bulgaria, Romania, Serbia, Montenegro, Macedonia, and Kosovo, with plans to expand into Bangladesh and other Asian countries as a springboard for future Global Engagement activities in the Middle East. CEED assists entrepreneurs by offering training, consulting, and business networking services in three areas: entrepreneurial growth, access to finance, and developing new markets. Of particular note, CEED operates "Top Class," a one-year training program aimed at helping young entrepreneurs under 35 years old develop the skills they need to grow operations. The program combines training in response to leadership, marketing, and financial issues, as well as a mentorship program that gives budding entrepreneurs access to proven, successful entrepreneurs. CEED is a well-recognized initiative, earning accolades as a major contributor to SME development and receiving a Distinguished Service Group Award from USAID for its innovative approach to promoting entrepreneurship.

---

[6] Wim Naude, "Promoting Entrepreneurship in Developing Countries: Policy Challenges." Policy Brief No. 4, UNU-WIDER. 2010.
[7] Gorman, Gary, Dennis Hanlon and Wayne King. 1997. "Some Research Perspectives on Entrepreneurial Education, Enterprise Education and Education for Small Business Management: A Ten-year Literature Review." International Small Business Journal 13/3 (April-June): 56-.

Another example of the USG's efforts towards promoting entrepreneurship is the Global Entrepreneurship Program (GEP). Although entrepreneurship has always been of utmost importance for the United States, in terms of both foreign policy and its impact on trade and job creation, it has received increased attention by the Obama administration in recognition of its ability to transform societies and improve the livelihoods of people throughout the world. Established in April 2010, GEP is a U.S. Department of State initiative, comprising a coalition of 119 private sector, university, non-profit organizations, and individuals, whose mission is to spur the development of entrepreneurial ecosystems in target countries by providing a platform for collaboration between its partners and the USG. The inherent strength of GEP as an organization resides in the wide spectrum of products, services, information, and contacts available to entrepreneurs from its partner organizations.

Designing an Entrepreneurship Program: Best Practices

The ability to design and implement a successful entrepreneurship program requires careful planning and oversight to ensure It brings about the anticipated impact required for sustainable entrepreneurial ecosystem improvement. To achieve this, USG officers need to not only clearly define the pillars of entrepreneurship to include within their program, but also attain a good understanding of the drivers or conditions that exist within their respective country that directly influence the proliferation of entrepreneurs.

Designing an Entrepreneurship Program

1. Define the scope of assistance in terms of funding available
2. Ascertain the receptivity of key stakeholders to the proposed program
3. Identify the entrepreneur target group

In determining project scope, USG officers should always consider the amount of funding available to implement entrepreneurship assistance activities. Dependent upon funding, entrepreneurship programs may include all of the six pillars of entrepreneurship outlined in this toolkit, or may need to be tailored or scaled back to include only one single component. This is an important point to make, since providing tangible assistance to entrepreneurs can, and in certain cases should, occur outside the framework of a large-scale, comprehensive entrepreneurship implementation program. For example, entrepreneurs may benefit greatly from receiving only training or provision of a mentor. Of course, this is not to say that assistance in all six areas is not necessary or potentially more effective, but instead reinforces the fact that the most important step in strengthening entrepreneurs' capacity is to prioritize those components best suited to meet their most pressing needs in a fiscally conservative manner.

USG officers also need to carefully weigh how implementation of an entrepreneurship program will affect public and private-sector organizations and individuals, as well as any potential ramifications that may occur within the overarching business-enabling environment. The importance of this cannot be overstated, in that the best intentions of such a program can be quickly lost if the audience is resistant to or not ready for the changes associated with implementation. As such, it is often recommended to build a portfolio of champions, within government institutions, private sector businesses, and NGOs willing to vocalize their support to help build public consensus for the program and help manage expectations. Furthermore, it is also to allow the project to make necessary adjustments based on feedback from target group recipients when early stage program interventions are planned on a pilot basis.

Lastly, USG officers must be attuned to the variation of potential entrepreneur types and groups that exist when designing a program. For example, there should be a clear decision made as to the age, socio-economic status, geographic location, and type of entrepreneurs to include when developing strategies and actions for the projected program to ensure objectives are aligned and realistic.

Summary of Best Practices and Lessons Learned

When you are working to *Identify* entrepreneurs...

- Align entrepreneur identification with project objectives and anticipated funding sources.
- If working with a pre-selected group of enterprises, it is best to draw on the recommendations of incubators and entrepreneurial communities on the ground, rather than attempting to set criteria and conduct the selection itself.
- Allow entrepreneurs to self-select in programs aimed at increasing the number of growth entrepreneurs assisted.
- Support projects that provide platforms or literally physical locations where entrepreneurs can meet and be introduced to investors, organizations, networks, and support systems they can leverage.
- Communication of minor improvements from judges and mentors to entrepreneurs during business plan competitions can, in the long-term, create a more robust entrepreneurial ecosystem.

When you are working to *Train* entrepreneurs...

- Even at an elementary school level, it is possible to equip students with skills in creative thinking and problem-solving that they will require as entrepreneurs later in life.
- Explore ways to link U.S. universities with foreign-based universities to facilitate knowledge transfer and improvements to curriculum development.
- Capacity building of entrepreneurs outside the formal education system (e.g., soft skill and technical training) is a critically important task towards building a solid entrepreneurial ecosystem.
- Education and training alone are necessary but insufficient without providing other kinds of support, such as mentorship, connections to funding (especially for growth entrepreneurs) and financial assistance (for micro-entrepreneurs).

When you are working to *Connect and Sustain* entrepreneurs...

- A high degree of trust must exist between a mentor and protégé to maximize the effectiveness of the arrangement.
- Mentors who possess a wide breadth of business knowledge are typically more effective in this role than technical specialists, since entrepreneurs often need advice on a wide range of topics.
- High-profile entrepreneurs bring additional clout and recognition to any entrepreneurship assistance program, but it is important to confirm their commitment and availability.
- Linkages between mentors and protégés from the same country work best.
- Videoconferencing works better than phone calls, yet there is no substitute for the opportunity to at least periodically meet in-person.
- Skill-based mentoring is most effective when an entrepreneur is matched with a mentor from the same industry.
- Entrepreneurs need to be connected, not only to mentors but also to each other.

When you are working to *Fund* entrepreneurs...

- Venture capital is, in most cases, not a binding constraint for entrepreneurs. Projects should focus more on facilitating access to seed and angel funding.
- In order to actualize targeted funding, aim to identify growth entrepreneurs who could ultimately employ dozens or hundreds of employees, rather than only a handful. It is these types of entrepreneurs who will eventually fuel economic growth.

- Access to traditional loans can be accomplished by supporting banks in areas such as structuring and preparing loans for SMEs, providing collateral through funds such as USAID's Development Credit Authority, and supporting the formation of credit bureaus.
- Developments in virtual platforms, software and psychometric tools represent an excellent opportunity to quickly and effectively identify, assess, and link entrepreneurs with investors and financial institutions throughout the world.
- Funding the "missing middle" can prove very beneficial. Often times the overstated strengths of microfinance cloud the need for slightly larger amounts of funding – even $10,000-$20,000 – could make huge differences to slightly larger entrepreneurs.

When you want to *Enable* the business environment for entrepreneurs...

- Reducing bureaucracy is important in encouraging informal entrepreneurs to formally register.
- Initiatives designed to lower bureaucratic obstacles in order to encourage registration of informal entrepreneurs should be accompanied by an information campaign designed to make such entrepreneurs aware of the changes.
- For growth entrepreneurs, policy changes in other less obvious areas may actually have an equal or greater impact. For example, stronger anti-monopoly policies will increase the number of perceived opportunities and can lead to greater entrepreneurial activity.

When you want to promote the culture of and *Celebrate* entrepreneurs...

- Celebrating success is an important contributor to mindset change and can be effectively done through media events and highly publicized awards, as well as government literature, speeches, and interviews.
- Showcasing entrepreneurs may best occur as part of highly-attended conferences and conventions to generate a stir among the audience and ensure ample visibility for the entrepreneur.
- Word-of-mouth promotion is often the most effective yet least expensive tool to proselytizing entrepreneurs.
- Tailor the choice of entrepreneurs or successes to highlight in accordance with the profile of the audience. Remember that local (native) examples are more powerful and relevant to an audience.
- Do not forget to include smaller organizations both as examples to showcase and as invitees. While "big names" may generate interest, the enthusiasm and excitement of smaller firms may easily spread to a large segment of the entrepreneurial population.

When you want to do any *combination* of the six key areas above...

- Programs to support entrepreneurship, and in particular incubators, should, as often as possible, pair funding and linkages to support networks with training activities.
- Make sure there is a suitable and appropriate management structure in place prior to making any investment.
- Donor-created incubators often do not work efficiently nor do they prove to have sustainable impact.

Identify

Best Practices

The identification of promising entrepreneurs should always begin with an understanding of the objective a program is hoping to achieve, in order to align program objectives with target entrepreneurs and reach expected results. Some programs aim to provide employment for the many individuals who do not have easy access to a job, either because of gender or the inability of the private sector in any given country to create them. Other programs attempt to stimulate innovation and large-scale employment by working with high-growth entrepreneurs who have identified a clear market niche and are actively trying to transform into what is commonly defined as "gazelles," defined by David Birch as small, rapidly growing companies with annual sales revenue growth of 20% or more for four consecutive years which create substantial job opportunities.[8]

Development of a burgeoning group of motivated entrepreneurs is a requirement for societies that wish to continue sustained economic growth. Although this is a shared objective of organizations working in the field of entrepreneurship development, the methods used to attract entrepreneurs and the type selected significantly vary. In regard to actual identification, BGI discovered four methods typically employed by organizations: business plan competitions, social events, training, and marketing/word-of-mouth.

Perhaps the most visible activity to garner interest from entrepreneurs is hosting a business plan competition, in which entrants submit their formalized business ideas, in hopes of being selected to receive a monetary prize, meet potential investors or, in the best scenario, a combination of both. Not only does this activity, as historically proven, pique considerable interest, it also serves an additional function of publicizing or celebrating the success of profiled entrepreneurs (see Celebrate for more information). Furthermore, the range of entrepreneurial ideas brought forward for consideration can be easily tailored, based on the parameters associated with the competition (i.e., narrowing the base of ideas by specifying an industry or widening it to include ideas from any business discipline).

There are other events, whether they be more technical in nature, such as entrepreneur workshops or roundtables, or social, such as "meet and greet" networking functions, that may also draw significant participation. A key element in organizing such an event is promotion and informing the right target audience, which should include not only entrepreneurs, but also possible investors, since their presence nearly guarantees attendance.

While training is itself a separate component of entrepreneurship improvement, it does provide organizations an excellent opportunity to meet entrepreneurs. Those that are most effective at using this approach are keenly aware of the usefulness of training participant data and capitalize on this opportunity by developing collection methods (e.g., participant registration forms) that capture the scope and depth of information needed to gauge and plan for future cooperation. This method yields even greater gains if the organization hosting the training has solid ties to another set of actors - investors and mentors - to build potential linkages between the two parties.

Additionally, many organizations have developed a strong reputation in the market, and as such are in the enviable position of constantly attracting potential entrepreneurs through referrals (word-of-mouth). As such, these firms may not often face the common obstacle of quantity, but must instead spend significant time and effort identifying the quality or type of entrepreneurs to assist.

---

[8] Hot Industries, Cognetics Inc., Cambridge, Massachusetts, 1995

Resource List

Case Studies

- AllWorld Network: Visibility Economics and the Tipping Point
- Endeavor: The Quest for High-Impact Entrepreneurship
- TechnoServe: Transforming Ideas into Improved Livelihoods

Key Questions for Program Design

Lessons Learned for Future USG Assistance

Entrepreneurship Development Firm Contact List

- AllWorld Network
- Endeavor
- The Hatchery
- Microsoft Egypt
- TechnoServe

USAID Project Summary: Country Guide

- Afghanistan
- Albania
- Armenia
- Azerbaijan
- Bahrain
- Bangladesh
- Belarus
- Bosnia
- Bulgaria
- Cambodia
- Central Asia (region-wide)
- East Africa (region-wide)
- Egypt
- El Salvador
- Georgia
- Global

- Haiti
- Herzegovina
- India
- Indonesia
- Iraq
- Jordan
- Kazakhstan
- Kenya
- Kosovo
- Kuwait
- Kyrgyz Republic
- Kyrgyzstan
- Lebanon
- Liberia
- MENA (region-wide)
- Middle East (region-wide)

- Moldova
- Mongolia
- Morocco
- Oman
- Philippines
- Pakistan
- Paraguay
- Qatar
- Swaziland
- Tajikistan
- Thailand
- Turkey
- Turkmenistan
- United Arab Emirates
- Ukraine
- Uzbekistan

- West Bank/ Gaza
- Yemen
- Zambia
- Zimbabwe

Publications/Reference Materials

Case Studies

AllWorld Network: Visibility Economics and the Tipping Point

AllWorld Network was established in 2007 by Deirdre Coyle, Anne Habiby, and Michael Porter. Its objective is to create the largest information system and network of growth entrepreneurs in the world, to achieve what Ms. Habiby calls the "Facebook of economics." AllWorld is translating this objective into a reality through identification, ranking and dissemination of the 500 fastest growing companies (as measured by revenue growth instead of size) in Arabia, Africa, Asia, Eurasia, and Latin America.

AllWorld Network at a Glance

AllWorld Network was established in 2007. Its objective is to create the largest information system and network of growth entrepreneurs in the world. AllWorld is translating this objective into a reality through identification, ranking and dissemination of the 500 fastest growing companies, as measured by revenue growth instead of size, in Arabia, Africa, Asia, Eurasia, and Latin America.

Contact:
Anne Habiby; ahabiby@allworldlive.com

Its business model is built on the premise that developing economies do not lack a sufficient number of entrepreneurs in operation, but instead suffer from those entrepreneurs not having enough visibility to investors and customers. This results in massive market inefficiencies, with investors throughout the world identifying and competing for the same funding opportunities from a limited pool of companies. Such restrictions ultimately lead to a holistic reduction in the level of capital infusion needed to spark a country's economic growth. AllWorld seeks to address this problem through what it terms "Visibility Economics," meaning the ability to increase exposure to the right companies that will drive investors to them and lead to increased funding. AllWorld strives to achieve a "Visibility Tipping Point" in which enough well-positioned, high-growth companies receive the visibility they need to reach domestic and even international impact in scaling growth and job creation.

Companies that wish to be considered must apply via AllWorld's website (www.AllWorldLive.com). Upon receipt, AllWorld evaluates each organization's competitive capacity and reviews its three-year history of annual revenue growth. After doing so, AllWorld compiles a ranking of the top 500 for the region, with the fastest growing company ranked first, and followed by each successive company in descending order. Those without the three-year financial track record required can qualify as "Companies to Watch." The importance of being selected as a top 500 performer rests in the increased visibility that comes from this data being distributed on a global basis through social and traditional media. Savvy investors consistently seek out opportunities for investment in financially sound "up and comer" companies, which AllWorld readily provides to the global community.

Although it operates as a for-profit business, most of AllWorld's current activities, essentially publication of their rankings, are paid for by corporate sponsors. Ultimately it hopes to use the information it has access to through publication of these rankings, to identify investment-worthy companies through the creation of venture capital, private equity, and joint venture funds, as well as business services.

In many ways, USG collaboration with AllWorld could parallel that with Endeavor, in that both organizations focus on high-impact or growth entrepreneurs. The USG could use "word-of-mouth" marketing to build awareness of its mission and objectives to encourage entrepreneurs meeting AllWorld's criteria to apply for inclusion into its rankings. Additionally, it could use AllWorld's annual rankings to identify and select a cadre of the fastest growing companies in each target country to showcase during entrepreneurship celebratory and promotional events, as well as serve within a mentoring capacity.

Endeavor: The Quest for High-Impact Entrepreneurship

Endeavor is a non-profit organization, founded in 1997 by Linda Rottenberg and Peter Kellner, whose mission is "leading the global movement to catalyze long-term economic growth by selecting, mentoring, and accelerating the best High-Impact Entrepreneurs around the world." The uniqueness of Endeavor as an organization is its targeted approach to providing assistance to entrepreneurs it defines as high-impact; those being a very small group of "exceptional entrepreneurs who run innovative, high-growth businesses that create thousands of jobs, millions in wealth, and limitless opportunity in their countries."

Endeavor's mission is translated into action very visibly, through the rigorous approach it takes to developing its pool of high-impact entrepreneurs. Endeavor uses a three-pronged approach to identifying candidates, comprised of proactive research by Endeavor staff, recommendations garnered from its network of affiliates, and self-nomination by entrepreneurs via Endeavor's website.

After an initial screening of thousands of entrepreneurs each year, Endeavor selects only those that they believe have the right potential to proceed to the interview process. Endeavor staff conducts an initial hour-long interview to assess each potential candidate's viability before passing those deemed appropriate on to senior-level VentureCorps (Endeavor's network of business professionals) representatives who conduct multiple interviews with each candidate on multiple topics, including their business strategy, potential for growth, and interpersonal qualities.

> *Endeavor at a Glance*
>
> Endeavor is a non-profit organization, founded in 1997 whose mission is "leading the global movement to catalyze long-term economic growth by selecting, mentoring, and accelerating the best High-Impact Entrepreneurs around the world."
>
> Contact:
> David Wachtel; david.wachtel@endeavor.org

Those candidates selected to advance are then interviewed by 10-15 VentureCorps and local Board Member staff who decide which candidates to recommend for a final review by an Endeavor Managing Director and financial expert. The interview process culminates in a unanimous vote by affiliate international business leaders to approve a new class of Endeavor entrepreneurs.

As Endeavor President Fernando Fabre noted, the selection process takes an average of 12-18 months, with approximately 4% of potential candidates chosen as "Endeavor entrepreneurs." This level of rigor is put in perspective when considering, as noted in Endeavor's 2009-2010 Impact Report that, "Harvard Business School selected just over 10% of applicants for the class of 2011."

Endeavor's rationale for adoption of this strategy is correlated to how company size directly affects gross domestic product (GDP). For example, as noted in its 2009-2010 Annual Report, achievement of a 1% increase in GDP in Mexico would require the creation of 449,900 micro-firms, 20,064 small firms, 984 medium firms or 85 large firms. This marked difference in the scope of companies necessary to establish to create this type of change is at the core of Endeavor's allocation of resources to entrepreneurs.

When asked to further justify Endeavor's approach, Fernando noted, "A common misconception of most entrepreneurship programs is a single-minded focus on 'quantity' rather than 'quality'." He further explained that although the inherent intent of nearly all assistance programs is positive – in that they are undertaken to improve the livelihoods of those in the country by increasing salaries and creating jobs – trying to actively help a large swath of potential entrepreneurs typically "waters down" what could have been achieved with a more targeted approach (e.g., focusing solely on high-impact entrepreneurs).

While there is certainly credence in this as demonstrated by the statistics above, BGI understands there is a difference between what Endeavor is capable of and the assistance typically provided by the USG, which traditionally aims to support both need-based entrepreneurs and high-impact entrepreneurs. Also, while Endeavor seeks the next "big" entrepreneur, the USG alone cannot cost-effectively achieve its objective of promoting entrepreneurship on a worldwide basis. However, it is important to acknowledge the large ripple effect high-impact entrepreneurs can have with respect to both GDP and job creation.

As such, designers and implementers of entrepreneurship programs should consistently look for ways to include organizations like Endeavor, its contact network, and its group of high-impact entrepreneurs. For example, the USG could create employment opportunities by trying to link entrepreneurs that complete USG-supported training as potential employees for recipient firms run by Endeavor entrepreneurs. As stated above, Endeavor's entrepreneurs operate the type of high-growth businesses that require a constant flow of well-qualified staff, making this type of initiative well-aligned with and complementary to USG objectives. Another option is to include Endeavor's entrepreneurs as speakers or panelists during USG-funded entrepreneurship conferences or delegations. Their presence could prove to be a significant boon to such events, in that they serve as shining examples of the type of entrepreneurs many aspire to become. Lastly, the USG could use Endeavor's entrepreneurs as role models or mentors, to help a broader group of entrepreneurs learn from their experiences and adopt the same or similar principles that have brought them success.

TechnoServe: Transforming Ideas to Improved Livelihoods

Founded in 1968, TechnoServe currently works in over 30 countries and has over 1,000 employees. Entrepreneurship is at the core of TechnoServe's operations. As Brian Phillips, Global Entrepreneurship Director, remarked, it is the "engine that drives economic growth in countries throughout the world. Entrepreneurs' ability to create jobs and bring about actual improvement in people's lives is clearly documented and should be more fully celebrated."

TechnoServe at a Glance

TechnoServe is an international development organization whose mission is to reduce poverty in developing countries by providing entrepreneurs with the skills, knowledge and contacts needed to build businesses that create income, opportunity and growth for their families, communities and countries.

Contact:
Brian Philips; BPhillips@tns.org

TechnoServe actively seeks to improve the livelihoods of enterprising men and women in developing countries by building their capacity to effectively translate their ideas into action. One method TechnoServe uses to create a roster of entrepreneurs is to host business plan competitions. Due to its effectiveness, TechnoServe has hosted these events in 18 countries including India, Africa and Central and South America during the past decade. While use of this type of competition is well-established, TechnoServe's position is somewhat unique in that it strives to positively impact all participating entrepreneurs, not just the best performers in the competitions. By enlisting the help of local representatives from businesses, government and academia, TechnoServe solicits business plans from entrepreneurs on a national basis. All participants of these competitions are provided with training to help them improve the overall quality of their business plans. As importantly, each participant is given the opportunity to network with key stakeholders from the local entrepreneurship ecosystem. The most promising participants are then chosen to advance through the program. They receive feedback on their proposed plans, as well as intense training and personal mentoring. Following another round of evaluation, judges select finalists, who receive continued post-competition mentoring, linkages to potential capital sources, and vouchers for additional business support services. The winners of each competition also receive a seed capital grant in addition to the aforementioned assistance. TechnoServe did an impact assessment of their Central American work with entrepreneurs and demonstrated that over a two-year period, the after-care participants generated a 150% increase in sales and a 150% increase in jobs, mobilized 200% additional capital, and were twice as likely to still be in business, relative to nonparticipants who were not part of the program.

TechnoServe already has a well-established relationship with USAID as a project implementer in many developing countries. It believes very strongly in the need for any organization, including the USG, to take a long-term perspective (e.g., at least 5-10 years) when implementing entrepreneurship development programs. Critical success factors for such interventions include: role modeling by successful entrepreneurs to stimulate interest and ambition; the provision of feedback and coaching to a wide swath of entrepreneurs; targeted assistance to those better positioned to translate the feedback into actual action; and strengthening the ecosystem of committed local financiers, investors, and business development service providers ready to support the emerging entrepreneurs. Support for longer term programs designed to catalyze systemic changes in the attraction of entrepreneurship as a vocation, as well as the realization that emerging entrepreneurs can access training and support from local business leaders and the establishment of the supporting ecosystem on a sustainable basis are very much aligned with the USG's objective to attain "reach" within the countries in which it works. It should be an inherent principle in any future USG-supported initiatives aimed at transformative private sector development. The USG would benefit from working with TechnoServe to expand the number of business plan competitions currently held in its target countries, as well as expand these events into other areas of the world. Additionally, the USG, through sponsorship, could devise additional competitions that are more targeted in terms of industries represented or an increased focus on rural entrepreneurs.

Key Questions for Program Design

- What is the expected duration of the project?
- What is the scope of your planned assistance efforts (number of entrepreneurs)?
- Do you have an estimated amount budgeted for identifying entrepreneurs? If yes, how much?

- Is there a particular focus on:
  - Age?
  - Gender?
  - Economically disadvantaged entrepreneurs?
  - Minority entrepreneurs?
  - Rural or urban-based entrepreneurs?
  - Specific industries?
  - First-time entrepreneurs?
  - Entrepreneur type (i.e., "high-impact" entrepreneurs, "missing middle" entrepreneurs, etc...)
- If yes, what special consideration will be given and how will recruitment efforts ensure this objective is met?

- Which media will you use to identify entrepreneurs?
  - Websites
  - Newspaper
  - Radio
  - Television
  - Referrals
  - Word-of-Mouth
- Do you have estimated costs for the applicable advertising media?

- How will you monitor and report on the identification of entrepreneurs?
  - Number of entrepreneurs receiving USG assistance
- How will you disaggregate entrepreneurs identified?
  - By age
  - By gender
  - By socio-economic status
  - By geographic location
  - By industry
  - By type

Lessons Learned for Future USG Assistance

1. Align entrepreneur identification with project objectives and anticipated funding sources. For instance, for anti-poverty programs, entrepreneurial micro-enterprises (including youth, women and minority populations) are an appropriate target and microfinance is a likely (and appropriate) source of funding. For programs that focus on job creation, growth entrepreneurs are a better target, while more appropriate sources of funding might include angel, seed, and venture capital. Projects that aim to create jobs depend on this type of entrepreneur and may necessitate prioritizing this group. This finding is reinforced by the Global Entrepreneurship Monitor's report that concluded only 14% of start-ups expect to create 20 jobs or more.

2. In cases where the USG wants to work with a pre-selected group of enterprises, it is best to draw on the recommendations of incubators and entrepreneurial communities on the ground, rather than attempting to set criteria and conduct the selection itself.

3. In programs where the USG wants to increase the number of growth entrepreneurs assisted, rather than working only with a smaller, more targeted group, it is better to allow entrepreneurs to self-select. This should be done by creating opportunities, such as replicable businesses models, instead of trying to engineer the process by attempting to identify entrepreneurs or to turn necessity entrepreneurs into growth entrepreneurs.

4. Support should be given to projects that provide platforms or literally physical locations where entrepreneurs can meet and be introduced to investors, organizations, networks, and support systems they can leverage. The USG could use a number of different ways to incentivize those from the entrepreneurial ecosystem to attend, including organizing a business plan competition; hosting a conference featuring high-level, keynote speakers; or offering speed-networking events. Regardless of the method chosen, the end goal is to ensure that entrepreneurs have the opportunity to present their business ideas and concepts in a way that will promote networking between themselves and potential investors and mentors.

5. Incorporation of minor improvements communicated by judges and mentors to entrepreneurs during business plan competitions can, in the long-term, create a more robust entrepreneurial ecosystem. Such feedback should be available to as many entrepreneurs as possible to create a "multiplier effect."

Entrepreneurship Development Firms Contact List

Organization	Contact Name	Email	Website	Focus Area(s)
AllWorld Network	Anne Habiby, Co-Founder	ahabiby@allworldlive.com	www.allworldlive.com	Identify (*Primary*) Connect & Sustain; Celebrate (*Secondary*)

Organization Summary

AllWorld Network was established in 2007 by Deirdre Coyle, Anne Habiby and Michael Porter with the objective to create the largest information system and network for growth entrepreneurs in the world; described as the "Facebook of economics." AllWorld is translating this objective into a reality through identification, ranking and dissemination of the 500 fastest growing companies (as measured by revenue growth instead of size) in Arabia, Africa, Asia, Eurasia, and Latin America. AllWorld operates under the premise that developing economies do not lack a sufficient number of entrepreneurs, but instead suffer from those entrepreneurs not having enough visibility to investors and customers. To address this problem, a central tenet of the organization, termed "visibility economics," is that entrepreneurs should be more visible in order to attract investors.

Organization	Contact Name	Email	Website	Focus Area(s)
Endeavor	Fernando Fabre, President	Fernando.fabre@ endeavor.org	www.endeavor.org	Identify *(Primary)* Connect & Sustain; Celebrate *(Secondary)*

Organization Summary

Founded in 1997, Endeavor is a non-profit organization dedicated to fostering high-impact entrepreneurship on a global basis. High-impact entrepreneurship is defined as identifying and supporting the continued growth of a select group of entrepreneurs in emerging market countries, creating jobs and adding revenues that would lay the groundwork for a new attitude toward entrepreneurship in each respective country. Endeavor's mission is to transform emerging countries by establishing high-impact entrepreneurship as the leading force for sustainable economic growth. Endeavor helps high-impact entrepreneurs in 11 countries (mostly focused on Latin America and the Middle East) unleash their potential by providing an unrivaled network of business leaders to act as mentors and provide strategic advice/inspiration. Their business model is built on five elements: launch, select, support, multiply, and give back.

Organization	Contact Name	Email	Website	Focus Area(s)
The Hatchery	Yao-Hui Huang, Co-founder and Managing Partner	yao@hatchery.vc	www.hatchery.vc	Identify *(Primary)* Connect & Sustain; Train; Celebrate *(Secondary)*

Organization Summary

The Hatchery is a venture collaboration organization committed to building communities of entrepreneurs, investors, corporations, academia, and associations through events, advisory, and venture acceleration. The events at the heart of The Hatchery model provide a platform for innovators to interact with a wide range of funders and founders, present their plans, receive expert feedback, build up an all-start team, and pave the way towards receiving angel and institutional funding. This organization also provides venture acceleration encompassing pitching, financial analysis, strategic development, and incubation. The Hatchery has a presence in eight countries and 10,000 people in its affiliated network.

Organization	Contact Name	Email	Website	Focus Area(s)
Microsoft Egypt	Sherif Abbas, DPE Lead	sherifa@microsoft.com	http://www.microsoft. com/en/eg/	Identify *(Primary)* Train *(Secondary)*

Organization Summary

Microsoft Egypt has partnerships with the Egyptian government in various areas, including entrepreneurship. The company usually trains and offers price cuts on software to entrepreneurs/startups that will belong to Microsoft's ecosystem. On certain occasions, they train fresh graduates from major universities and even professors of those universities. Their reasoning for providing assistance programs is that they help build a reliable ecosystem that will use Microsoft products.

Organization	Contact Name	Email	Website	Focus Area(s)
TechnoServe	Brian Phillips, Global Entrepreneurship Director	BPhillips@tns.org	www.technoserve.org	Train *(Primary)* Train; Connect & Sustain *(Secondary)*

Organization Summary

TechnoServe is a development assistance organization whose mission is to help entrepreneurial men and women in poor areas of the developing world build businesses that create income, opportunity, and economic growth for their families, their communities, and their countries. Founded in 1968, TechnoServe works in more than 30 countries and has more than 1,000 employees. Work is concentrated primarily in the agriculture and agribusiness, tourism, and alternative energy sectors. To achieve its objectives, TechnoServe utilizes a three-pronged technical approach: empower entrepreneurs in developing countries to capitalize on good business opportunities; build businesses and industries by focusing on further developing thriving SMEs; and improve the business environment by improving access to capital (via financial institutions) and leadership development (via its role in ANDE).

Back to Top - Identify   *Back to Resource List – Identify*

Train

Best Practices

Entrepreneurship training is a widely debated topic and has been the subject of lively discourse. While there is no clear consensus, there are many voices, both in favor of and against the notion that it is possible to, in fact, "make" an entrepreneur. The central point of disagreement is not so much on training entrepreneurs – for instance, in improving their ability to write a business plan or preparing financial projections, which most agree is of use – but instead the ability to actually develop an individual's entrepreneurial spirit; in other words, teaching people the intangible elements (e.g., willingness to take risks, ability to make strategic decisions with limited information, etc…) which entrepreneurs typically possess. This is exemplified by the phrase that "entrepreneurs are born, not made" and helps explain why many working in this field are more interested in spending time and resources to ensure the enabling environment is conducive to business.

> ### Elements to Consider When Training Entrepreneurs
>
> 1. *Format:* classroom instruction vs. virtual delivery
> 2. *Subject:* soft skills vs. technical
> 3. *Scope:* breadth vs. depth

Among the most robust supporters of entrepreneurship training BGI identified are Babson College, the Kauffman Foundation, and INJAZ Al-Arab (a member of Junior Achievement Worldwide). Their stance is further strengthened from the results of a study conducted by the Monitor Company. By interviewing entrepreneurs from 22 countries across multiple regions and different levels of economic development, Monitor found a greater correlation exists than previously believed between the teaching of entrepreneurial skills and entrepreneurship performance.

The structure and delivery of entrepreneurship training is most commonly divided between in-person and virtual courses. The choice of which form to use is also substantially influenced by the scope of the desired assistance, with on-line training being the method utilized to reach a much larger target audience. Typically, BGI found that in-person training was more often chosen in the teaching of soft-skill subjects, such as negotiating skills, since it requires identification and adoption of more subtle verbal cues and communication.

Entrepreneurship training is no longer reserved for those at a university or post-university age, which is beginning to gain more traction, but is instead occurring across age ranges. For instance, HighScope in Indonesia teaches entrepreneurship skills to elementary-aged students, while INJAZ focuses on imparting skills and knowledge to those between the ages of 14 to 21 years old.

Entrepreneurship training programs may also be very narrow in the selection of the target group, based on entrepreneur type, socio-economic status, or geographical location; one example is the Education for Employment Foundation, which tailors its courses to help unemployed or disadvantage youth in several countries in the Middle East and North Africa.

Resource List

Case Studies

- Babson College: The Entrepreneurship Method and Positive Deviance
- Education for Employment: Providing Skills to Build Careers
- Global Business School Network: Teaching to Teach Entrepreneurs
- Global Social Benefit Incubator: Social Entrepreneurs with a Proof of Concept
- INJAZ al-Arab and HighScope: Molding Future Entrepreneurs

Key Questions for Program Design

Lessons Learned for Future USG Assistance

Entrepreneurship Development Firm Contact List

- American University in Cairo
- AMIDEAST
- Babson College
- Education for Employment Foundation
- Egyptian Junior Business Association/Middle East Council for Small Business and Entrepreneurship
- E-Learning Competence Center
- Extreme Entrepreneurship LLC
- Global Business School Network
- Global Social Benefit Incubator
- Hewlett-Packard
- High Scope Indonesia
- INJAZ al-Arab
- Institute of International Education
- Nile University
- Potential
- Technology, Innovation, and Entrepreneurship Center
- William Davidson Institute

USAID Project Summary: Country Guide

- Afghanistan
- Albania
- Armenia
- Azerbaijan
- Bahrain
- Bangladesh
- Belarus
- Bosnia
- Bulgaria
- Cambodia
- Central Asia (region-wide)
- East Africa (region-wide)
- Egypt
- El Salvador
- Georgia
- Global

- Haiti
- Herzegovina
- India
- Indonesia
- Iraq
- Jordan
- Kazakhstan
- Kenya
- Kosovo
- Kuwait
- Kyrgyz Republic
- Kyrgyzstan
- Lebanon
- Liberia
- MENA (region-wide)
- Middle East (region-wide)

- Moldova
- Mongolia
- Morocco
- Oman
- Philippines
- Pakistan
- Paraguay
- Qatar
- Swaziland
- Tajikistan
- Thailand
- Turkey
- Turkmenistan
- United Arab Emirates
- Ukraine
- Uzbekistan

- West Bank/ Gaza
- Yemen
- Zambia
- Zimbabwe

Publications/Reference Materials

Case Studies

Babson College: The Entrepreneurship Method and Positive Deviance

Entrepreneurship at the university level has received increasing attention in the United States and elsewhere. Babson College is well-recognized as a leading school for entrepreneurship in the United States, offering students the opportunity to study cutting-edge, innovative techniques from highly-esteemed faculty. Babson summarizes the tenets of its entrepreneurship program as "a mindset that is opportunity obsessed, holistic in approach, and leadership balanced." It describes its classrooms as "living laboratories," and has established a comprehensive entrepreneurship education framework through development of new value creation, social entrepreneurship, entrepreneurship finance, technology, and public policy curricula. Babson's approach focuses on teaching entrepreneurship as a "method." Instead of relying on case studies and business plans as the foundation of curricula, Babson requires students to start and close a real business, using games and simulations to learn how to think under conditions of extreme uncertainty and ambiguity. Additionally, Babson has developed content that targets a wide range of entrepreneurs, including start-ups, those interested in growing their business, and niche groups such as youth and women.

Babson College at a Glance

Babson College is recognized as the leading school for entrepreneurship in the United States, offering students the opportunity to study cutting-edge, innovative techniques from highly-esteemed faculty. Babson summarizes the tenets of its entrepreneurship program as "a mindset that is opportunity obsessed, holistic in approach, and leadership balanced."

Contact:
Donna Kelley; dkelley@babson.edu

In the summer of 2010, Babson formalized its relationship with the Abu Dhabi School of Management, established by the Abu Dhabi Chamber of Commerce and Industry, to create a new school focused on using entrepreneurship as the core driver of its business program. As a leader in this field, Babson will provide its expertise into all aspects of this new school, to ensure it meets international accreditation standards. Dr. Shahid Ansari, Provost of Babson, believes wholeheartedly that entrepreneurship can in fact be taught and that educating entrepreneurs at all levels is critical. Dr. Ansari compared teaching the principles of entrepreneurship to the scientific method; by stating "not all students of entrepreneurship will become entrepreneurs, just like not all students who learn the scientific method will become scientists." Among other things, Dr. Ansari points out, Babson teaches what is known as positive deviance – an approach to behavioral and social change based on the observation that in any community, there are people who will utilize uncommon but successful behaviors or strategies that enable them to find better solutions to a problem than their peers, despite facing similar challenges and having no extra resources or knowledge than their peers. For example, cases in which one or two people didn't suffer from a water-borne illness in a village and looking at what they did differently. A key element of this approach involves teaching budding entrepreneurs to ask three questions when devising a potential solution: Who am I?, What do I know?, and Who do I know?

Dr. Ansari recommends that the USG should not attempt to direct entrepreneurial efforts on the ground, but instead effectively act as a referee by setting the rules of the game; meaning, use its obvious clout and leverage to improve enabling environment factors such as the legal system and property rights. The USG could also support capacity building through educating entrepreneurs by providing matching funds to help broaden Babson's scope of assistance. This modest contribution could prove extremely productive, considering the current level of interest expressed by professors at Babson who are prepared to volunteer their time. Lastly, Dr. Ansari recommends the USG not focus efforts on trying to create corporate spin-offs, since they are a natural by-product of entrepreneurial activity. As he noted, "The problem with incubators isn't the incubators themselves; it's that an environment that doesn't focus entrepreneurs on answering the right three questions leads to the incubation of bad ideas."

Education for Employment Foundation:
Building Futures Through Youth Employment Across the Middle East and North Africa

Education for Employment (EFE) is a network of locally-run, affiliated not-for-profit organizations that provide young people in the Middle East and North Africa (MENA) with tools and opportunities to start a job, build their future and give back to communities. EFE creates job opportunities for unemployed youth in the MENA region by providing world-class professional and technical training that leads directly to jobs.

By garnering the support of business, government, education and civic leaders, EFE creates locally-run non-profits. EFE affiliates are currently in Morocco, Yemen, Jordan, Egypt, Palestine and most recently, Tunisia. Each EFE affiliate is locally-run and partially locally-funded. This ensures that each affiliate works as an efficient and sustainable model. Affiliates leverage resources and best practices through the EFE global network, and EFE shares the governance in each foundation with distinguished local leaders, providing guidance and project management support through its U.S. offices and sister foundation in Europe, EuropEFE. EFE, EuropEFE, and EFE affiliates cooperate in fundraising and program implementation. To play a greater role in advocating change across the region, EFE actively helps local academic institutions, employers and NGOs replicate its internationally recognized programs. These public-private partnerships ensure that thousands more youth benefit from education and employment opportunities that EFE designs.

Education for Employment
at a Glance

The Education for Employment (EFE) Foundation is a training-based network of affiliate organizations whose mission is to provide disadvantaged youth, those limited by socio-economic constraints or inadequate education, with the right mix of skills and knowledge to gain employment and build careers.

Contact:
Jasmine Nahhas di Florio;
jnahhasdiflorio@efefoundation.org

EFE is distinct in its role linking unemployed youth with businesses in need of well-qualified staff. EFE identifies sectors of the economy that offer solid potential for growth and job creation but lack appropriately-qualified personnel. In conjunction with businesses that promise to hire EFE graduates, innovative training courses are created that are directly linked to jobs. Aside from providing "soft skills" such as communications, leadership, teamwork, and interviewing techniques, EFE tailors the courses and content offered according to the types of positions companies are seeking to fill. This customization can result in a wide range of topics offered, from banking to land surveying to hotel management to teaching. Through customization, EFE ensures that the needs of partner companies are met by providing highly prepared graduates for employment.

EFE also has a strong emphasis on placing participants into jobs, placing nearly 80 percent of its graduates since 2004. Nearly 50% of EFE's graduates are female, addressing gender inequality in the workforce. The region's female labor force participation rate of 26% is well below the 39% average for Low and Middle Income countries. EFE also offers graduates continued support through mentoring and alumni networks. Alumni are connected with like-minded peers who offer them support in their new jobs and help them to become engaged citizens.

While EFE has only recently launched this component, it is well-positioned to translate the gains it has already made by linking aspiring entrepreneurs with individuals and organizations that can serve as mentors and foster success. The U.S. Government could reap significant benefits, not only through more direct interaction with EFE, but from adoption of EFE techniques when developing training programs in the future.

Global Business School Network: Teaching to Teach Entrepreneurs

The Global Business School Network (GBSN) is a nonprofit whose mission is to promote business and management education worldwide. Founded on the concept that too few SMEs in developing countries have well-trained managers, GBSN was created as a unit at the IFC and now is a stand-alone organization. They aim to network business schools overseas and in the U.S., their faculty members, private consultants, the private sector and governments to provide training and capacity building to entrepreneurs in the areas of management, strategic planning, entrepreneurship, and business skills.

GBSN works with business schools all over the world include ones such as the Karachi School for Business and Leadership in Pakistan, Kenyatta University in Kenya, University of Ibadan in Nigeria, and Moshi University College of Cooperative and Business Studies in Tanzania. Schools like these collaborate with GBSN in many facets, including generating local teaching materials and curriculum, establishing or strengthening specific courses (e.g. entrepreneurship, business skills and management, agribusiness), or working with GBSN to connect to other institutions or those in their community to strengthen their programs. GBSN also works primarily in the agriculture, business, entrepreneurship, health, and tourism sectors.

GBSN at a Glance

The Global Business School Network (GBSN) is a nonprofit whose mission is to promote business and management education worldwide. They aim to network business schools overseas and in the U.S., their faculty members, private consultants, the private sector and governments to provide training and capacity building to entrepreneurs in the areas of management, strategic planning, entrepreneurship, and business skills.

Contact:
Guy Pfefferman; info@gbsnconnect.org

GBSN engages its worldwide network of top business schools to promote management education that combines international best practices with local relevance. Chief Executive Officer Guy Pfeffermann notes that one of the most important things to do when conducting a training course of developing an institution in an emerging market is to "tailor it as closely as possible to the region, country, city, or culture. Do something that is local…give them actual cases they can understand, and show them success stories they can relate to." GBSN does just that by forging collaborative partnerships between local leaders and international experts to create high-quality training programs specific to market needs. The result is a new class of business-savvy entrepreneurs creating jobs in their communities and contributing to the economic and social development of their countries.

Pfeffermann also encourages people to "only work where there is very strong demand – do not push it where it isn't wanted or where they aren't ready for it." In that vein, the USG has a unique opportunity to collaborate with GBSN. Various Missions or Embassies overseas have the best positioning and knowledge of their local environments. Should any Mission or Embassy already know of academic centers or universities who have expressed the need for increased training in GBSN's core focus areas, they would be an ideal partner with which to connect. Beyond the training and curriculum development they offer, they can also connect lesser known universities overseas to stronger ones in the U.S. and elsewhere, who can provide sound advice, networking, and learning opportunities to help other universities strengthen and grow. Utilizing their on-ground knowledge and any contacts or networks at universities, the USG can point different universities or schools to GBSN for strengthening and support.

Global Social Benefit Incubator: Social Entrepreneurs with a Proof of Concept

The Global Social Benefit Incubator (GSBI™) is the flagship entrepreneurship program of Santa Clara University's Center for Science, Technology and Society (CSTS). Established in 2003, GSBI™ selects and provides leadership training for an extremely diverse group of professionals from all over the world , whom it deems "social entrepreneurs;" those who who clearly demonstrate a desire to address fundamental human or societal problems in a systematic, collaborative manner to realize transformational change. In selecting trainees, GSBI™ looks for a "proof of concept" that shows that the idea underpinning the enterprise has been tested in the field, has demonstrated positive impacts on clients, is unique, and has potential economic viability. Specific emphasis is put on the role of mentoring as a way to complement formal business training with informal knowledge and support, customized to the participants' individual needs.

The purpose of this program is to help enable social entrepreneurs and their respective organizations to effectively overcome obstacles to "scale up." This is done through a combination of four months of distance preparation with mentors prior to a two-week and in-residence training program. Social entrepreneur's experience at GSBI™ culminates with development of a summary business plan presentation to Silicon Valley entrepreneurs and venture capitalists.

Global Social Benefit Incubator at a Glance

The Global Social Benefit Incubator (GSBI™) is the flagship entrepreneurship program of Santa Clara University's Center for Science, Technology and Society (CSTS). GSBI works with an extremely diverse group of professionals from all over the world of "social entrepreneurs." GSBI™ looks for a "proof of concept" that shows that the idea underpinning the enterprise has been tested in the field, has demonstrated positive impacts on clients, is unique, and has potential economic viability.

Contact: Eric Carlson; ecarlson@scu.edu

Since inception, GSBI™ has had 138 award-winning social entrepreneurs attend its program and can report that over 50% of its alumni report that their impact and income are increasing at a rate greater than their expenses. The USG, through cooperation with GSBI™, could develop or support activities geared towards improving the ability for social entrepreneur's success, particularly considering the pressing need and importance of attaining cross-tangible impact in areas such as increasing literacy, basic health care services, environmental practices, and sanitation.

INJAZ al-Arab and HighScope: Molding Future Entrepreneurs

INJAZ at a Glance

INJAZ aL-Arab, a member of Junior Achievement Worldwide, is based in Amman, Jordan and is a union of national organizations operating in 13 countries across the Middle East and North Africa whose mission is to "help inspire a culture of entrepreneurialism and business innovation among Arab youth."

Contact:
Soraya Salti; Soraya@injaz-arabia.org

INJAZ al-Arab, a member of Junior Achievement Worldwide, is based in Amman, Jordan and is a union of national organizations operating in 13 countries across the Middle East and North Africa whose mission is to "help inspire a culture of entrepreneurialism and business innovation among Arab youth." The bulk of its efforts go towards building the capacity of youth aged 14-21.

The foundation of its program is in building the capacity of its targeted youth through the provision of business-related skills training. This includes a combination of soft-skill instruction, through modules such as work, career, life skills training, and business ethics, as well as training in more technical subjects as entrepreneurship, economics, and financial literacy.

INJAZ al-Arab is uniquely positioned as the only organization in the MENA region that provides business training as part of the educational curriculum, and (similar to the Education for Employment Foundation) focuses on providing youth with a broad mix of skills and knowledge needed to successfully find employment in the marketplace upon graduation. In addition, it has hosted the INJAZ al-Arab Young Entrepreneurs Competition the past four years, an event that brings students from throughout the Arab world to compete in acquiring awards given out for the "most innovative product," "best marketing plan," "best company of the year," and "young entrepreneur of the year." INJAZ al-Arab's programs have been very well received and have achieved impressive results demonstrated through reaching over 900,000 youth and engaging 10,000 volunteers since its inception in 2004.

HighScope Indonesia was established in 2000 and offers preschool, elementary, middle school and high school programs for children aged 1½ to 18 years old. HighScope believes that a school is a learning organization that involves everyone in the system – students, parents, educators, community leaders, government officials, and business people who express their aspirations, build their awareness, and develop their capabilities together by learning from one another.

The challenge is to change the mindset of people who would rather work for someone else than start a business; 80% of college graduates with bachelor degrees would choose to work for an established company. "You need to teach individuals to not be afraid of starting a business and you need to do so from childhood," says Antarina Amir, Managing Director of HighScope Indonesia. This is a principle that the school she manages is focused on: building the confidence of students by encouraging creativity and calling for persistence - qualities that, among others, drive entrepreneurial success. "It is very important for Indonesian students to see successful entrepreneurs who are Indonesians themselves", says Antarina. Successful local entrepreneurs can serve as good examples and can promote local entrepreneurship in a country that has abundant natural resources and high potential for entrepreneurial activities.

> **HighScope at a Glance**
>
> HighScope, was established in 2000 and offers preschool, elementary, middle and high school programs for children aged 1½ to 18 years. HighScope teaches business skills and encourages students to engage in entrepreneurial activities.
>
> Contact:
> Siti Maidatun Naimah; frd@highscope.or.id

Highscope also helps high school students develop their confidence and self-esteem. They currently host an annual Business Plan Challenge for HighScope High School students where the students present their business plans as one of the requirements for their Virtual Enterprise course. The Virtual Enterprise course is a simulated business model where the students run a virtual company consisting of a CEO, managers and various department heads the same as in a real life company. They buy, sell, and advertise on-line using virtual currency with their counterparts all over the world. The business presentations during this Challenge are judged by a panel of business practitioners, who, at the end of the Challenge, conduct a rigorous question and answer session.

Currently, Antarina conducts the Business Plan Challenge in one school only as a pilot project; however, in the future she plans to increase the number of participating high schools and conduct competitions, similar to the competitions in the U.S. and Europe. Consequently, she is in the process of planning the expansion of this program to motivate the participating students to consider entrepreneurship as a life choice and personally encounter a close to real-life experience in setting up businesses and working as entrepreneurs.

In addition, HighScope teaches business skills in elementary and middle school and inspires students to engage in entrepreneurial activities. These young HighScope students either sell their own creative arts (paintings and models, etc.) or resell agricultural produce. This enables them not only to apply the sales techniques they learn in school, but also to understand the more complex business concepts of pricing, profit making, and retention of profits. Some students use the proceeds from their sales to share their success with less fortunate children through charity activities. An important takeaway from this exercise is that students learn persuasion skills, persistence and responsibility, and gain confidence that they can earn money by themselves and decide how that money will be used.

As youth training providers, INJAZ al-Arab and HighScope could be useful partners for the USG. For example, both organizations would be excellent vehicles for cross-collaboration programs designed and implemented by USAID's Economic Growth and Education departments. Ideas for collaboration include linking both USG officials working in these countries, other project implementers and business leaders to serve as volunteers to help promote these programs. Furthermore, the USG could play a part in helping "celebrate" INJAZ al-Arab's and HighScope's award recipients by showcasing their profiles and, as applicable, inviting them to participate in other entrepreneurship events (e.g., conferences, delegations, etc.).

Key Questions for Program Design

Budget	• What is the scope of your planned assistance (number of entrepreneurs to train)? • Do you have an estimated amount budgeted for training entrepreneurs? If yes, how much? • Have you established a cost per unit for conducting training? If yes, how much?
Entrepreneur Target Group	• Where will you find entrepreneurs to train? • Educational institutions (colleges, universities, technical schools, etc...) • Professional associations • Virtual forums • Events (conferences, exhibitions, etc...) • Referrals from other organizations
Training Format	• What type of format will you use to train entrepreneurs • In-person (classroom instruction) • Virtual • Both
Communications	• How will you advertise training? • Websites • Newspaper • Radio • Television • Referrals • Word-of-Mouth • Do you have estimated costs for the applicable advertising media?
Monitoring and Evaluation	• How will you monitor and report on the identification of entrepreneurs? • Number of entrepreneurs receiving USG assistance • Number of courses delivered • How will you disaggregate entrepreneurs identified? • By age • By gender • By socio-economic status • By geographic location • By industry • By type

Lessons Learned for Future USG Assistance

1. Entrepreneurship education can be best supported by program funding at all levels of the educational system. Even at an elementary school level, it is possible to equip students with skills in creative thinking and problem-solving that they will require as entrepreneurs later in life.

2. Entrepreneurship training programs offer an excellent opportunity for joint coordination between USAID's Economic Growth and Education offices.

3. Exploring ways to link U.S. universities with foreign-based universities can be an important source of knowledge transfer and a way to leverage resources.

4. Capacity building of entrepreneurs outside the formal education system (e.g., soft skill and technical training) is a critically important task towards building a solid entrepreneurial ecosystem.

5. Education and training alone are necessary but insufficient without providing entrepreneurs with other kinds of support, such as mentorships, connections to funding (especially for growth entrepreneurs), and financial assistance (for micro-entrepreneurs).

Entrepreneurship Development Firms Contact List

Organization	Contact Name	Email	Website	Focus Area(s)
American University in Cairo (AUC)	Ghada Hafez, EIP Program Manager	gmhafez@aucegypt.edu	www.aucegypt.edu	Train *(Primary)* Connect & Sustain; Celebrate *(Secondary)*

Organization Summary

The Entrepreneurship and Innovation Program (EIP), is offered through AUC's School of Business, in recognition of the importance of fostering entrepreneurship in Egypt. EIP, since its inception in October 2010, has held over 20 events to date, including business plan competitions, training in finance, marketing, and business plan development; has launched a virtual platform (www.wamda.com) to connect entrepreneurs, innovators and thought leaders; has participated in the ArabNet (http://arabnet.me/roadshow/) Road Show; has promoted social entrepreneurship through the Global Social Venture Competition (www.gsvc.org); and is currently establishing an incubator innovation center. Of particular note, ten to twelve percent of entrepreneurs EIP works with have either been accelerated or taken up by other companies.

Organization	Contact Name	Email	Website	Focus Area(s)
AMIDEAST	Ted Katouff, President and Chief Executive Officer	mlozny@amideast.org	www.amideast.org	Train *(Primary)* Connect & Sustain *(Secondary)*

Organization Summary

AMIDEAST is a MENA-focused development organization that aims to expand educational opportunities and quality, strengthen the capacity of local institutions, and help students develop the language and professional skills required to succeed. It does this primarily through cultural and academic exchanges, most notably through implementation of its Fulbright Foreign Student Program.

Organization	Contact Name	Email	Website	Focus Area(s)
Babson	Donna Kelley, Associate Professor of Entrepreneurship	dkelley@babson.edu	www.babson.edu/eship	Train *(Primary)*

Organization Summary

Babson is a leading school for entrepreneurship in the United States. Its' Arthur M. Blank Center focuses on expanding the practice of entrepreneurship through innovative co-curricular programs and global collaborative research initiatives that inspire and inform entrepreneurial thought and action. Outside the classroom, students "live" entrepreneurship through the comprehensive Babson Venture Accelerator, over a dozen student-run entrepreneurship organizations and forums, and the Boston-area entrepreneurial ecosystem. They recently developed a relationship with the Abu Dhabi School of Management, and plan to use the partnership to set up a center of entrepreneurship there.

Organization	Contact Name	Email	Website	Focus Area(s)
Education for Employment (EFE) Foundation	Jasmine Nahhas di Florio, Vice President, Strategy and Partnerships	jnahhasdiflorio@efefoundation.org	www.efefoundation.org	Train *(Primary)* Connect & Sustain *(Secondary)*

Organization Summary

The Education for Employment (EFE) Foundation is a training-based network of affiliate organizations whose mission is to provide disadvantaged youth (those limited by socio-economic constraints or inadequate education) with the right mix of skills and knowledge to gain employment and build careers. EFE achieves this by working with representatives from the business, education, governmental and civic and community sectors in Egypt, Jordan, Morocco, West Bank/Gaza, Yemen, and most recently, Tunisia, to create partnerships that produce job commitments for its program constituents. As a training provider, EFE offers both soft-skill (e.g., workplace success professional skills) and technical (e.g., accounting, sales) training to ensure its participants have a well-rounded skill base to apply in future positions.

Organization	Contact Name	Email	Website	Focus Area(s)
Egyptian Junior Business Association (EJBA) / Middle East Council for Small Business & Entrepreneurship (MCSBE)	Amr Gohar	agohar@ntccegypt.com	www.ejb.org.eg/ www.mcsbe.org/	Train *(Primary)* Fund; Celebrate; Enable *(Secondary)*

Organization Summary

MSCGE is an NGO and affiliate of the International Council for Small Business which hosts about 100 stakeholders, educators, researchers, and others from the financial sector and focuses on culture, policy/ strategies, know-how development, and financing. MSCGE is also involved in Global Entrepreneurship Week, provides research support by publishing the Global Entrepreneurship Monitor, and conducts the USAID-funded Entrepreneurship Education Initiative.

EJBA has two primary activities: capacity building in universities, offering training in English and entrepreneurship concepts; and finance to entrepreneurs through a grant of 1.25M Egyptian pounds. Over the past two years, they have financed industry loans to 10-20 entrepreneurs.

Organization	Contact Name	Email	Website	Focus Area(s)
E-Learning Competence Center (ELCC)	Yasser Kazem	ykazem@mcit.gov.eg	www.elcc.gov.eg	Train *(Primary)* Connect & Sustain *(Secondary)*

Organization Summary

The E-Learning Competence Center (ELCC) focuses on education/training/capacity building through the use of e-learning technology in Egypt. It is part of the Ministry of Communications and Information Technology, and also works in cooperation with Cisco. ELCC's most direct impact with entrepreneurship is the work that they do to support SMEs. Additionally, ELCC has developed the Egypt Entrepreneurs Network, an online portal where entrepreneurs can interact and network.

Organization	Contact Name	Email	Website	Focus Area(s)
Extreme Entrepreneurship, LLC	Michael Simmons, Founder	michaeldsimmons@gmail.com	www.extremee.org	Train *(Primary)* Connect & Sustain *(Secondary)*

Organization Summary

Extreme Entrepreneurship, LLC is a New York-based media and education company, dedicated to helping college students plan, prioritize, and pursue their own vision in life by utilizing the entrepreneurial mindset. It was founded by two NYU students who knew that many speaker series existed to inspire students to become entrepreneurs, but gave few concrete directions on how to start their own businesses. Extreme Entrepreneurship aims to fill that void, and delivers tours and programs to high school and university students in the United States. They deliver a keynote speaker series and virtual sessions, offering training on how to write a business plan, network, seek mentors, and develop stronger business acumen. The organization also recently launched a virtual business incubator.

Organization	Contact Name	Email	Website	Focus Area(s)
Global Business School Network (GBSN)	Guy Pfeffermann, Chief Executive Officer	info@gbsnconnect.org	www.gbsnonline.org/	Train *(Primary)* Connect & Sustain *(Secondary)*

Organization Summary

The Global Business School Network (GBSN) is a non-profit whose mission is to promote business and management education worldwide. Founded on the concept that too few SME's in developing countries have well-trained managers, GBSN was created as a unit at the IFC and now is a stand-alone organization. They work to network business schools overseas and in the U.S.; their faculty members, private consultants, the private sector and governments provide training and capacity building to universities in management, strategic planning, entrepreneurship, and business skills.

Organization	Contact Name	Email	Website	Focus Area(s)
Global Social Benefit Incubator (GSBI), Santa Clara University	Eric Carlson, Director	ecarlson@scu.edu	www.scu.edu/ socialbenefit	Train *(Primary)* Connect & Sustain *(Secondary)*

Organization Summary

The Global Social Benefit Incubator (GSBI) is the signature program of Santa Clara University's Center for Science, Technology and Society (CSTS). It works with social entrepreneurs to empower them and their organizations to overcome barriers to scale and impact. The program works in three phases: online application exercises, four months of distance preparation with executive mentors, and a two-week in-residence program at Santa Clara University involving intense executive education and mentoring sessions, culminating with formal business plan presentations to Silicon Valley entrepreneurs and venture capitalists. Since inception, GSBI™ has had 138 award-winning social entrepreneurs attend its program.

Organization	Contact Name	Email	Website	Focus Area(s)
Hewlett Packard (HP)	Sara Agarwal	sara.agarwal@hp.com	www.hp.com/hpinfo/ globalcitizenship/ 09gcreport/society/ social/entrepreneurship .html	Train *(Primary)* Celebrate; Fund *(Secondary)*

Organization Summary

Hewlett-Packard (HP) is a leading, global technology company operating in over 170 countries throughout the world to provide innovative business solutions and products to its clients. HP has an entrepreneurship education program, targeted primarily at 22-50 year olds, that involves the incorporation of technology into entrepreneurship training. HP works to deliver this training through NGOs (such as EDC) and is engaged with them in joint curriculum development.

Organization	Contact Name	Email	Website	Focus Area(s)
Highscope Indonesia	Siti Maidatun Naimah	frd@highscope.or.id	www.highscope.or.id	Train *(Primary)*

Organization Summary

Highscope Indonesia (HSI) endeavors to be the world's innovator and barometer of education in Indonesia, through teacher training and curriculum development programs. It operates within Indonesia and has grown from Jakarta to Bandung, Denpasar, and Medan. HSI is seeking to establish a virtual enterprise to educate Indonesian students in business, entrepreneurship, finance, economics, and technology. Kindergarten-aged students learn business concepts, while 9-10 year olds in the program develop business plans. HSI actively encourages a new generation of entrepreneurs through a task-based curriculum and hands-on activities.

Organization	Contact Name	Email	Website	Focus Area(s)
INJAZ Al-Arab (Junior Achievement – MENA)	Soraya Salti, Regional Director	soraya@injaz-arabia.org	www.injaz.org.jo	Train *(Primary)* Connect & Sustain *(Secondary)*

Organization Summary

INJAZ Al-Arab, based in Amman, Jordan and operating in 14 Arab countries, runs programs for 14-21 year olds (the majority being 14-17) to provide them with practical, hands-on business education. INJAZ is based on an "education for employment" model and manages three separate programs: entrepreneurship, workforce readiness (critical thinking, problem-solving, time management, teamwork, etc.), and financial literacy. Their programs depend on grants from private sector firms, some of which include Citibank, Deloitte, HSBC and MasterCard. INJAZ uses a corporate board of about 220 members drawn from the private sector who volunteer to teach the content of the courses. The organization believes its value-add is that these volunteers also teach, providing a practical element to the courses and allowing them to serve as role models. INJAZ is also starting an entrepreneurship reality television series titled "Generation Entrepreneur" to change the mindset of Arab youth and motivate them to become entrepreneurs themselves. Furthermore, it will initiate funding of student start-ups that demonstrate real-world potential with help from corporate partners serving as mentors and, as applicable, providing angel funding.

Organization	Contact Name	Email	Website	Focus Area(s)
Institute of International Education (IIE)	Wagaye Johannes, Assistant Director, Global Scholarship & Learning Programs	WJohannes@iie.org	www.iie.org	Train *(Primary)* Connect & Sustain *(Secondary)*

Organization Summary

The Institute of International Education (IIE) is a non-profit that focuses on education worldwide, primarily through scholarships, grants, and training. They administer some of the world's most well-known scholarships, such as the Fulbright. They also provide for many learning opportunities, such as study tours and internship opportunities for young students to travel or work in the U.S. to get hands-on learning.

Organization	Contact Name	Email	Website	Focus Area(s)
Nile University (NU)	Dr Tarek Khalil, University President	info@nileuniversity.edu.eg	www.nileu.edu.eg	Train *(Primary)* Identify; Connect & Sustain *(Secondary)*

Organization Summary

Nile University (NU) is a non-profit educational institution whose mission is to contribute to the development of the technology-driven economies in Egypt and the region through the pursuit of education and research at the highest levels of excellence. Nile University operates both an undergraduate and graduate program. In fostering entrepreneurship, NU arranges mentorships, holds business plan competitions, and manages the Enterprise Competitiveness and Innovation Center.

Organization	Contact Name	Email	Website	Focus Area(s)
Potential	Shadi Banna, Owner	info@potential.com	www.potential.com/uae	Train *(Primary)* Connect & Sustain *(Secondary)*

Organization Summary

Potential offers training (primarily on-line) to two groups of entrepreneurs: start-ups, and those that have started small enterprises and are looking to expand their existing businesses. The majority of their focus is on the latter group. Their training, which they call "SME Evolution," is a three-month program that focuses on topics such as marketing, sales, human resources, and finance. They conduct most of the training themselves (with in-house resources), although they occasionally use other partners. For the most promising enterprises, both start-ups and organizations looking to grow, Potential offers skills coaching through which they connect members of their organization on a one-to-one basis with these entrepreneurs. Potential started in Qatar, the UAE, Oman, and Lebanon and are looking to expand to other MENA countries in the future.

Organization	Contact Name	Email	Website	Focus Area(s)
Technology, Innovation, and Entrepreneurship Center (TIEC, formerly ITIDA)	Ahmed Liaili	Alaiali@tiec.gov.eg	www.itida.gov.eg	Train *(Primary)* Fund *(Secondary)*

Organization Summary

TIEC is a state-run incubator that provides entrepreneurship education, awareness, competitions, PPPs, and funding (angel and seed capital). They emphasize working with those in high-tech, but are also interested in agribusiness. TIEC typically works with each enterprise for a period of two years, although under certain circumstances (such as if one of their entrepreneurs is negotiating with investors or is negotiating a business deal), this time frame can be extended. Their target is a 50-60% success rate, with success defined as firms able to generate revenues or attract investment during their incubation period. A precondition for participation is the existence of a business plan, and industry experts are used to determine whether the plan and opportunity are adequate. Funding is provided for up to about $250,000 per project.

Organization	Contact Name	Email	Website	Focus Area(s)
William Davidson Institute, University of Michigan (WDI)	Amy Gillett, Director, Executive Education	gilletta@umich.edu	www.wdi.umich.edu	Train *(Primary)* Connect & Sustain; Enable *(Secondary)*

Organization Summary

WDI is a think tank that focuses on business and policy issues in developing countries. They do research and train entrepreneurs, business school students, and professors. Training programs range from four-day basic "boot camp" to six-month long trainings (42 days spread over six months). For longer trainings, WDI helps trainees analyze their market, develop a business plan, and get connected to sources of financing. The vast majority of their beneficiaries are micro entrepreneurs (2-10 employees); sometimes they include SMEs.

Back to Top - Train   ***Back to Resource List – Train***

Connect and Sustain

Best Practices

A critical element in entrepreneurship development is the ability to foster peer-to-peer connectivity, as well as establish solid mentor-protégé relationships. In both cases, knowledge transfer is achieved through the sharing of experience, skills, knowledge, and tools between parties; if done effectively, this leads to a more savvy, proficient community of entrepreneurs.

Mentorship Types

1. In-person
2. Virtual
3. Skill-based (technical experts)
4. Relationship-based (generalists)
5. In-country
6. International

Fostering interaction between entrepreneurs is a major focus for many of the organizations we interviewed and is most commonly achieved through knowledge management portals and virtual exchange platforms. The crux of increasing interaction between entrepreneurs is their ability to learn from another and, as feasible, make available non-proprietary products and/or services to a greater portion of the entrepreneurial community in which they work.

Mentorships were also noted by many interviewees as critical to sustaining the success of entrepreneurs. The biggest difference regarding mentoring was whether the arrangement was "skill" or "relationship"-based. Skill-based mentoring, as the name implies, focuses on the technical skills needed to be an entrepreneur, while relationship-based mentoring focuses more on developing the target entrepreneur's decision-making ability and providing a sounding board for their ideas. Skill-based mentoring tended to be the most common form used among organizations. However, it is interesting to note that while this form tended to be the most popular, it was not always regarded as the most effective. The primary reason for this is that generalists were sometimes viewed as more valuable mentors to novice entrepreneurs, since their skill base would be broad enough to permit provision of some insight or guidance into a number of business topics, in comparison to that of an expert. In addition, many entrepreneurs' most pressing and frequent problems are not technical (e.g., preparing an income statement), but instead operational and/or strategic (e.g., deciding when and if to hire more staff), in nature.

Resource List

Case Studies

- Austin Ligon (Founder and Former CEO of CarMax): High-Profile Entrepreneurs and "Giving Back"
- Civilian Research and Development Foundation: Once the Laboratory, Now the Market
- Gust: The Investor Relations Platform Powering Global Start-up Financing
- ImagineNations Network: Leading from Behind

Key Questions for Program Design

Lessons Learned for Future USG Assistance

Entrepreneurship Development Firm Contact List

- ArabNet
- Aspen Network of Development Entrepreneurs
- Austin Ligon (Founder and ex-CEO of CarMax)
- CDC Development Solutions
- Gust
- Ernst & Young
- IBM
- ImagineNations Network
- Intel
- Legatum Center for Development and Entrepreneurship-MIT
- Mowgli
- National Business Incubator Association
- U.S. Civilian Research and Development Foundation
- Young Entrepreneur Council

USAID Project Summary: Country Guide

• Afghanistan	• Haiti	• Moldova	• West Bank/
• Albania	• Herzegovina	• Mongolia	Gaza
• Armenia	• India	• Morocco	• Yemen
• Azerbaijan	• Indonesia	• Oman	• Zambia
• Bahrain	• Iraq	• Philippines	• Zimbabwe
• Bangladesh	• Jordan	• Pakistan	
• Belarus	• Kazakhstan	• Paraguay	
• Bosnia	• Kenya	• Qatar	
• Bulgaria	• Kosovo	• Swaziland	
• Cambodia	• Kuwait	• Tajikistan	
• Central Asia (region-wide)	• Kyrgyz Republic	• Thailand	
• East Africa (region-wide)	• Kyrgyzstan	• Turkey	
• Egypt	• Lebanon	• Turkmenistan	
• El Salvador	• Liberia	• United Arab Emirates	
• Georgia	• MENA (region-wide)	• Ukraine	
• Global	• Middle East (region-wide)	• Uzbekistan	

Publications/Reference Materials

Case Studies

Austin Ligon (Founder and Former-CEO of CarMax): High-Profile Entrepreneurs and "Giving Back"

Austin Ligon, founder and former CEO of Car Max, is a legendary entrepreneur whom has taken an active interest in promoting global entrepreneurship. Although not directly associated with an individual company or organization, per se, Ligon is still very much involved in the business community and continues to directly invest in a multitude of different ventures. Furthermore, he continues to generously donate his time, as demonstrated through his participation in the GEP-sponsored Egypt Delegation, to mentor potential and budding entrepreneurs.

The importance of Ligon's role in a global entrepreneurship program cannot be overstated. He is a highly respected and well-recognized figure, both in the United States and abroad, who possesses a wealth of experience gained from establishing and operating a vast automotive enterprise. This is supplemented by the fact that he is also a seasoned investor, who has repeatedly been able to identify and fund successful entrepreneurial initiatives.

Austin Ligon at a Glance

Austin Ligon, founder and former CEO of Car Max, is a legendary entrepreneur whom has taken an active interest in promoting global entrepreneurship. Although not directly associated with an individual company or organization, per se, Ligon is still very much involved in the business community and continues to directly invest in a multitude of different ventures.

Contact:
Austin Ligon; ligona@gmail.com

Another point to recognize is Ligon's interest and willingness, to, as he noted, "give back" to the entrepreneur community. He does this through providing his time as a mentor to others, as well as in his capacity as an angel investor. However, Ligon perhaps best summarizes his position as being a "voice to garner support for entrepreneurs' successes and the positive impact they have on society." He firmly believes entrepreneurs, whether operating in the United States or Egypt or Indonesia, need to be more fully celebrated, since they are nothing short of the economic engine of growth.

Lastly, Ligon correctly pointed out that while his affiliation with the GEP is pro bono, he still consistently seeks out new opportunities to fund that are in line with his investment objectives. As he noted, this type of arrangement can be categorized as "win-win-win," since it positively benefits GEP, through his inclusion as a member; entrepreneurs, through receipt of mentoring and in some cases funding; and he himself, through a trusted way to "volunteer", as well as remittances attained as a result of his direct investments.

When taking into consideration his experience and desire to facilitate real change for entrepreneurs, Ligon is easily identified as the right type of "spokesperson" for an entrepreneurship assistance program. While he obviously is not a typical entrepreneur, the USG should recognize that there are several others that share many of the same experiences and interests as Ligon. With this said, it would be very beneficial for the USG to more actively replicate this type of partnership, whether it be on a programmatic or even project-basis, to build a formidable portfolio of high profile entrepreneurs able to provide increased recognition in the marketplace, highly sought after feedback via mentoring arrangements, and potential financing. The USG should also seek to include high-profile individuals like Ligon to attend a USG-sponsored event in order to draw positive attention, not only to the event itself but also to entrepreneurship. High-net worth investors, successful entrepreneurs, or established businesspeople can help to incentivize entrepreneurs to collect and meet in one place, and inspire them to also pursue their ambitions of running their own business. The USG has a unique opportunity to leverage its resources to collaborate with individuals such as Ligon and include them in their effort to connect entrepreneurs.

Civilian Research and Development Foundation: Once the Laboratory, Now the Market

The Civilian Research and Development Foundation (CRDF) is an independent, non-profit organization that promotes international scientific and technical collaboration to promote peace and prosperity. Based in Arlington, Virginia, CRDF has offices in Moscow, Kiev, Almaty and Amman, and focuses on building modern scientific infrastructures that foster innovation, while at the same time developing linkages between scientists and entrepreneurs to transform technological advances for use as business and/or consumer applications.

CRDF plays an active role in infrastructure development by working to improve the conditions needed to conduct scientific research, including upgrading equipment and laboratory facilities and access to technical literature, to build the skill and knowledge base of scientists. Furthermore, CRDF uses research grants, training, and exchange programs to minimize the legacy of the Soviet system's adage of "science for science's sake," in that ideas and inventions developed in a laboratory are never being shared with those [entrepreneurs] capable of tailoring it to serve society at large.

CRDF's clear distinction with other firms engaged in "connecting and sustaining" entrepreneurs is their emphasis on working with scientists and entrepreneurs interested in bringing forth high-technology innovation. This targeted approach to assistance efforts is well justified, considering, as [former] CRDF Vice President Eric Novotny pointed out, the incredible impact technology currently has and will continue to have on a global basis (e.g., internet, mobile phones, etc.) in nearly all aspects of daily life. This is further reinforced by acknowledging that so many of the commercial devices and instruments available today, although brought to light through the efforts of entrepreneurs, were, in fact, conceptualized in laboratories and research institutions by scientists.

An obvious lesson to take away from CRDF's experience is the importance of bridging together two distinct groups, which through collaboration, bring to fruition incredible societal change. As Novotny summarized, entrepreneurship programs should not attempt to "make scientists, entrepreneurs, and entrepreneurs, scientists, but instead realize the inherent strengths of each and develop opportunities to increase interaction between them as often as possible." CRDF has already established a strong presence in an extremely scientifically proficient region of the world and continues to build upon its existing network of scientists and entrepreneurs that could be well leveraged by USG officials. Additionally, CRDF may serve as a resource for multiple USG agencies and/or departments, in that it also aims to re-train scientists previously employed in a military capacity (e.g., working to develop weapons of mass destruction) to utilize their skills and knowledge in the civilian sector. An example highlighting this has been CRDF's ability to train nuclear weapon technicians to work in the field of nuclear medicine. An important takeaway for the USG is to acknowledge CRDF's innovative way of bringing two industries together in order to develop entrepreneurship from within, rather than from the top-down. Because of the USG's depth and breadth, it has the opportunity to also connect many new players and organizations to collaborate and utilize their skills to promote new, innovative industries.

Gust: The Investor Relations Platform Powering Global Start-up Financing

Gust was founded by veteran entrepreneur David S. Rose to provide an easy and efficient way to link angel investors and venture capitalists with entrepreneurs throughout the world. Based in New York City, it currently has a presence in over 65 countries, through its affiliation with 750+ investor networks, and more than 35,000 investors registered on its online platform.

Gust at a Glance

Gust was founded by veteran entrepreneur David S. Rose to provide an easy and efficient way to link angel investors and venture capitalists with entrepreneurs throughout the world. Based in New York City, it currently has a presence in over 65 countries, through its affiliation with 750+ investment groups, and over 35,000 investors registered on its online platform.

Contact:
Mark LaRosa; mark@gust.com

Gust is distinctive in that it has very effectively created an investor network community through the development and dissemination of its industry-leading software, which provides a secure system to manage an organization's deal flow. By using its software package, investors are able to capture deals, process them through a customizable work-flow process and collaborate with other investors.

Its overall mission is to increase smart investments into high-growth, early stage companies and to advance their success by providing the trusted platform and collaboration tools for their success and ongoing management. Gust will empower skilled entrepreneurs, enabling them to find, collaborate and succeed with the smartest investors. It accomplishes this by identifying and assembling investment networks throughout the world via a single virtual platform, streamlining the funding process of entrepreneurs in need.

Gust is not a "matching" site per se. Its primary intention is to provide the underlying infrastructure for the entire early stage finance ecosystem. It is also unique in that it focuses primarily on the needs of both investors and entrepreneurs. As Mark LaRosa, Vice President of Sales and Strategic Partnerships noted, their strategy so far was based on the premise that "if you have a strong network of investors, the entrepreneurs will come." With the recent launch of Gust (and rebranding of Angelsoft), entrepreneurs can now count on the most complete tool set to manage their investor relations, completely integrated to the platform investors already utilize for deal flow and syndication. They can safely create their companies' investor relations site, containing all the information investors need to know when considering an investment opportunity. They can share their site with investors on the platform and beyond, to be automatically considered for funding. That effectively makes Gust the universal platform for all parties' needs in early-stage financing.

Gust regards entrepreneurship as the driver of economic growth and job creation and operates according to the belief that entrepreneurship is most successful when it focuses on creating market linkages between investors and "self-selectors" - those that would be entrepreneurs in any case - instead of trying to "make" entrepreneurs.

With an extremely large and prominent network of investors throughout the world, Gust offers a strategic partnership opportunity for the USG. By capitalizing on this, USG officials could quickly gain access to a powerful and important group of business leaders to gain invaluable insight into investment trends and industries of interest (e.g., internet/web services, clean technology). This could directly influence not only the design of entrepreneurship programs, but also provide USG officials a sounding board for their respective ideas before implementation.

ImagineNations Network: Leading From Behind

ImagineNations is a global alliance of entrepreneurs, private sector organizations, mentors, thought leaders and individuals who partner to connect and sustain entrepreneurs all over the world through mentoring and advisement. ImagineNations Network is a free online platform for entrepreneurs to connect to each other and to mentors and to utilize resources to strengthen their businesses. ImagineNations Network's mission is to connect as many people as possible to share ideas, lessons learned, best practices, and guidance for business development and entrepreneurship.

Beyond connecting entrepreneurs to each other and to mentors, ImagineNations Network also offers ample resources entrepreneurs can utilize and learn from. Broken down by country, one can find free, easy-to-use documents explaining how to write a business plan, manage accounting documents, and step-by-step guides to starting up and running a business in that country. A list of local services featuring local organizations that can provide support is also provided.

ImagineNations seeks to "lead from behind," meaning to follow the demand of their entrepreneurs, not to set it for them. They also aim to scale all of their programs and tailor them to the specific environments from which the entrepreneurs are coming and ensure that all entrepreneurs are matched with mentors from their country or region with similar histories or experiences to share. Many entrepreneurs still are unaware of the power and necessity of mentors.

> *Global Social Benefit Incubator at a Glance*
>
> ImagineNations Network is a free online platform for entrepreneurs to connect to each other and to mentors and to utilize resources to strengthen their businesses. ImagineNation Network's mission is to connect as many people as possible to share ideas, lessons learned, best practices, and guidance for business development and entrepreneurship.
>
> Contact:
> Alan Flesichmann;
> alan@ahfleischmann.com
> Stephanie Harrington;
> stefanie@imaginenations.org

ImagineNations was one of the first GEP partners, and was selected to host the e-mentor platform before GEP was formally founded. They interact very closely with the Obama administration and the State Department as a source for mentors and entrepreneurs to connect. They have had dozens of interactions and collaborations with GEP and the State Department and thousands of entrepreneurs and mentors now use their platform. Their uniqueness lies in their simplicity – they are easy to use, relevant, localized, and free – all benefits for any entrepreneur.

ImagineNations envisions a number of ways that the USG can leverage them or partner with them further. The State Department could continue to use their facilitating and convening powers to promote ImagineNations to entrepreneurs and mentors that they have access to worldwide. USAID could also leverage them from a funding standpoint, by partnering with them and funding some of the programs they have or by designing programs based around their existing structures. For example, ImagineNations is currently working with Gallup to survey entrepreneurs worldwide to examine their demand for entrepreneurial mentoring and services. USAID could design and implement a program based on their findings.

Key Questions for Program Design

Budget	• What is the scope of your planned assistance (number of entrepreneurs)? • Do you have an estimated amount budgeted for connecting and sustaining entrepreneurs? If yes, how much?

Mentorship	• Where will you find potential mentors?
	  • Volunteer organizations
	  • Professional associations
	  • American Chamber of Commerce
	  • Virtual forums
	  • Events (conferences, exhibitions, etc...)
	  • Referrals from other organizations
	• Are there specific characteristics associated with the mentoring program?
	  • Local/In-country mentors only
	  • Regional mentors acceptable
	  • International mentors acceptable
	  • Industry-specific
	  • Previous mentoring experience

Peer-to-Peer Connectivity	• Have you identified potential partners' virtual platforms to use to connect entrepreneurs? If yes, which?
	  • Local government
	  • Universities
	  • Associations
	  • Private-sector businesses
	  • Social networks
	• Will this program require building a website/virtual platform? If yes, how will this be achieved?

Monitoring and Evaluation	• How will you monitor and report on connecting and sustaining entrepreneurs?
	  • Number of mentor-protégé relationships established
	  • Number of website visits
	  • Number of online entrepreneur profiles created/ registered
	• How will you disaggregate entrepreneurs?
	  • By age
	  • By gender
	  • By socio-economic status
	  • By geographic location
	  • By industry
	  • By virtual platform type

Lessons Learned for Future USG Assistance

1. A high degree of trust must exist between a mentor and protégé to maximize the effectiveness of the arrangement, since to do so requires sharing and discussion of sensitive information, such as personnel issues and financial data. Building trust must be built over time and is best fostered by ensuring both parties are committed to the relationship and are clear of their respective roles.

2. Mentors that possess a wide breadth of business knowledge are typically more effective in this role than technical specialists, since entrepreneurs often need advice on a wide range of topics. This is especially true when considering most entrepreneurs' need for support in "day to day" operations.

3. High-profile entrepreneurs bring additional clout and recognition to any entrepreneurship assistance program, but it is important to confirm their commitment and availability.

4. Linkages between mentors and protégés from the same country often work best, considering the strong need for mutual understanding of cultural nuances and the business climate.

5. Videoconferencing works better than phone calls, yet there is no substitute for the opportunity to at least periodically meet in-person.

6. Skill-based mentoring is most effective when an entrepreneur is matched with a mentor from the same industry.

7. Entrepreneurs need to be connected, not only to mentors but to each other. Helping to establish support groups, networking events, or small group meetings is a productive way for the USG to get involved and promote collaboration and thought sharing. Often entrepreneurs can find comfort in the knowledge that there are others out there facing the same problems or obstacles.

Entrepreneurship Development Firms Contact List

Organization	Contact Name	Email	Website	Focus Area(s)
ArabNet	Omar Christidis, Founder	omar@arabnet.me	www.arabnet.me	Connect & Sustain *(Primary)* Train *(Secondary)*

Organization Summary
ArabNet's goal is to connect entrepreneurs with investors. With this aim in mind, ArabNet 2010 brought 500 top entrepreneurs using web/mobile content to the event to pitch their ideas to interested investors; in 2011 ArabNet attracted 1,000. This year ArabNet also conducted a road show, designed to train and inspire aspiring or established entrepreneurs across 7 countries in the region, including instruction on how to start a business, raise funds, identify market trends, and make a sales pitch. Additionally, they have created a hub (via a blog) for entrepreneurs to connect with one another, and started an Investor Corps, whereby entrepreneurs who submit interesting ideas may have them broadcast to interested investors.

Organization	Contact Name	Email	Website	Focus Area(s)
Aspen Network of Development Entrepreneurs (ANDE)	Jenny Everett, Associate Director	Jenny.Everett@aspeninst.org	www.aspeninstitute.org	Connect & Sustain *(Primary)* Celebrate; Train; Fund; Enable *(Secondary)*

Organization Summary

The Aspen Network of Development Entrepreneurs (ANDE) is a global network of 125 member organizations that invest money and expertise to propel entrepreneurship in emerging markets. ANDE has linkages with partners in 150 countries. Officially launched in 2009, they are a member-driven organization focused on small and growing businesses (SGBs) that create economic, environmental, and social benefits for developing countries. Ultimately, ANDE seeks to build sustainable prosperity in the developing world through strengthening "missing middle" entrepreneurs.

Organization	Contact Name	Email	Website	Focus Area(s)
Austin Ligon (CarMax Founder and ex-CEO)	Austin Ligon	ligona@gmail.com	Not applicable	Connect & Sustain *(Primary)* Fund *(Secondary)*

Organization Summary

Austin Ligon, founder and former CEO of Car Max, is a private, angel-stage investor and entrepreneur who has taken an active interest in promoting global entrepreneurship through his association with the Global Entrepreneurship Program. Specifically, he participated in GEP's Egypt Delegation and although not directly associated with an individual company or organization, per se, is still very much involved in the business community and continues to directly invest in a multitude of different ventures.

Organization	Contact Name	Email	Website	Focus Area(s)
CDC Development Solutions	Amanda MacArthur Director of Operations, Practice Leader, Global Citizenship and Volunteerism	amacarthur@cdc.org	www.cdc.org	Connect & Sustain *(Primary)*

Organization Summary

CDC Development Solutions is a non-profit organization that through its network of corporate and MBA Enterprise Corps volunteers helps strengthen entrepreneurs and SMEs to drive economic growth in emerging markets. To accomplish this objective, it relies on the establishment of innovative partnerships between the private, public, and social sectors to achieve sustainable growth in the areas of supply chain development, tourism, access to finance, and stability and economic recovery.

Organization	Contact Name	Email	Website	Focus Area(s)
Gust	Mark LaRosa, Vice President of Strategic Partnerships	mark@gust.com	www.gust.com	Connect & Sustain *(Primary)*

Organization Summary

Gust provides the global platform for the sourcing and management of early-stage investments. Gust enables skilled entrepreneurs to collaborate with the smartest investors by virtually supporting all aspects of the investment relationships, from initial pitch to successful exit. Gust is endorsed by the world's leading business angel and venture capital associations, and powers over 750 investment organizations in 65 countries. More than 125,000 startups have already used the platform to connect and collaborate with over 35,000 individual accredited investors. The company was founded in 2004 under the name Angelsoft and is privately held. Gust is based in New York, New York, with a development center in Vancouver, British Columbia, and European office in Paris, France.

Organization	Contact Name	Email	Website	Focus Area(s)
Ernst & Young LLP	Natasha Householder, Director Americas Communications & Marketing	Natasha.Householder @ey.com	www.ey.com	Connect & Sustain *(Primary)* Celebrate *(Secondary)*

Organization Summary

Ernst & Young (E&Y) is one of the premier consulting firms in the world in assurance, tax, advisory services and strategic growth markets. To help strengthen global entrepreneurship, E&Y is an active partner of the U.S. Department of State's E-Mentor Corps, which provides mentorships to entrepreneurs. In doing so, entrepreneurs gain access to a highly-esteemed corps of business leaders able to provide knowledge and skills, as well as share experiences, to help them successfully run their businesses. In addition, E&Y hosts its "Entrepreneur of the Year" award program, which selects and celebrates entrepreneur finalists and winners from one of ten industries.

Organization	Contact Name	Email	Website	Focus Area(s)
IBM	Robin Willner, Vice President Global Communities Initiatives	willner@us.ibm.com	www.ibm.com/ ibm/responsibility/ corporateservicecorpsibm/ responsibility/ corporateservicecorps	Connect & Sustain *(Primary)* Train *(Secondary)*

Organization Summary

IBM is a global technology services firm that regards its future success as inexorably tied to the progress of entrepreneurs. To foster entrepreneurship development worldwide, they have developed and launched an SME toolkit and operate the Corporate Service Corps, a program which sends delegations of IBM employees to emerging markets for four-week assignments to complete community-driven, economic development projects.

Organization	Contact Name	Email	Website	Focus Area(s)
ImagineNations Network	Alan Fleischmann, Managing Director Stephanie Harrington, Program Director	alan@ahfleischmann.com; stefanie@imaginenations.org	www.imagine-network.org	Connect & Sustain *(Primary)*

Organization Summary

ImagineNations Network is a global alliance of entrepreneurs, private sector organizations, mentors, through leaders and individuals who partner via an online platform to connect and sustain entrepreneurs all over the world through mentoring and advisement. ImagineNations Network's mission is to connect as many people as possible to share ideas, lessons learned, best practices, and guidance for business development and entrepreneurship. In doing so, ImagineNations seeks to "lead from behind," following the demand of their entrepreneurs rather than setting it.

Organization	Contact Name	Email	Website	Focus Area(s)
Intel Corporation	Carlos Contreras, US Education Manager	carlos.contreras@intel.com	www.intel.com/about/corporateresponsibility/education/highered/entrepreneurship.htm	Connect & Sustain *(Primary)* Train; Celebrate; Fund *(Secondary)*

Organization Summary

Intel is a leading technology company that aims to improve its customer's lives through the application of technologies, products, services, and initiatives. The Intel Higher Education program offers entrepreneurship programs designed to help move technology out of research labs and into local communities. They are currently working with US Berkeley faculty to create an entrepreneurship curriculum, and facilitate presentations by entrepreneurs to potential investors for prize money in Silicon Valley.

Organization	Contact Name	Email	Website	Focus Area(s)
Legatum Center for Development & Entrepreneurship at MIT	Iqbal Quadir, Founder and Director	legatum@mit.edu	http://legatum.mit.edu/	Connect & Sustain *(Primary)* Fund; Train *(Secondary)*

Organization Summary

The Legatum Center, founded in 2007, helps MIT students become entrepreneurs in developing countries, by providing ecological (connection to funders and innovators) and financial support (seed funding). It also hosts a lecture series and offers classroom training to students interested in starting a business. To date, the Center has graduated 55 students.

Organization	Contact Name	Email	Website	Focus Area(s)
Mowgli	Ian McKay, CEO	Ian.Mckay@mowgli.org.uk	www.mowgli.org.uk	Connect & Sustain *(Primary)*

Organization Summary

Mowgli connects entrepreneurs, primarily in the Middle East, with willing mentors. The nature of their mentorships is relationship, rather than skill-based, meaning they are looking to build the entrepreneur's ability to improve decision-making rather than offering specific expertise. Mentors do not need to be from the same industry, nor do they necessarily have the skills that would be identified as gaps by the entrepreneurs. Mentors fall into one of three categories: 1) those who are already engaged in developing leaders; 2) those who have been successful entrepreneurs themselves and are interested in giving back; or 3) people with a corporate profile who see this as a way of developing their own leadership and mentorship skills and are often encouraged by their companies.

Organization	Contact Name	Email	Website	Focus Area(s)
National Business Incubator Association (NBIA)	David Monkman, President & CEO	dmonkman@nbia.org	www.nbia.org	Connect & Sustain *(Primary)* Train *(Secondary)*

Organization Summary

NBIA is, in essence, an "incubator of incubators". As a reference for business incubators, it provides and disseminates research, consulting services, training, advocacy, and networking resources to business incubator managers and developers worldwide. NBIA also consults with government and corporations. Currently, it has more than 1900 members in 60+ nations (25% of its membership is outside the United States).

Organization	Contact Name	Email	Website	Focus Area(s)
US Civilian Research and Development Foundation (CRDF)		http://www.crdf.org/contact/	www.crdf.org	Connect & Sustain *(Primary)*

Organization Summary

The Civilian Research and Development Foundation (CRDF) is an independent, non-profit organization promoting international scientific and technical collaboration to promote peace and prosperity. Based in Arlington, Virginia, CRDF has offices in Moscow, Kiev, Almaty and Amman, and focuses on building modern scientific infrastructures that foster innovation, while at the same time developing linkages between scientists and entrepreneurs to transform technological advances for use as business and/or consumer applications. CRDF plays an active role in infrastructure development by working to improve the conditions needed to conduct scientific research, including upgrading equipment and laboratory facilities and access to technical literature, to build the skill and knowledge base of scientists.

Organization	Contact Name	Email	Website	Focus Area(s)
Young Entrepreneur Council	Scott Gerber, Founder	scottdgerber@gmail.com	www.theyec.org	Connect & Sustain *(Primary)* Train; Celebrate *(Secondary)*

Organization Summary

Scott Gerber is author of "Never Get a Real Job," and founder of the Young Entrepreneur Council (YEC), which connects entrepreneurs worldwide, delivering mentorship, growth support, promotion and celebration of entrepreneurship. YEC focuses on entrepreneurship as a method to create employment opportunities for youth and is a member-based organization. Its website offers users the opportunity to build their skills and knowledge via access to a broad range of entrepreneurship publications, as well as "Q+A" functionality through utilization of its advisory council.

Back to Top - Connect & Sustain   *Back to Resource List – Connect & Sustain*

Fund

Best Practices

Access to capital is regularly cited as, if not the most pressing, one of the most important requirements of creating a strong, high-functioning community of entrepreneurs. The ability to source financing is critical, as it serves as the lifeblood of any organization; however, a distinction must be made between equity capital necessary for growing firms and that needed to start them. As noted in the GEM study, 52% of entrepreneurs interviewed worldwide indicated there was sufficient equity capital to expand a firm's operations, while only 37% believed there was enough readily available to actually start a new business. The discrepancy being drawn is between venture capital and seed or angel capital. While venture capital is generally considered to be in adequate supply, and in fact unnecessary for a broad segment of entrepreneurs, gaining access to seed/angel capital is a more fundamental, critical need.

Another element to examine is the role of micro-finance and its impact on fostering entrepreneurship. Dufflo and Banerjee are the only the latest authors to find that while microfinance is a critical tool for micro-enterprises who lack access to finance at reasonable rates without some form of collateral, it is insufficient as a mechanism for supporting growth enterprises. In other words, while microfinance remains an important tool for supporting livelihoods, it is generally inadequate to drive large-scale job creation.

Furthermore, most entrepreneurs who graduate from microfinance find making the leap to the next step especially difficult. Banks, particularly those in developing countries, consider entrepreneurs at a slightly more advanced level not to be worth the credit risk. This is one explanation, and perhaps the most compelling, for the "missing middle;" economies that have many micro-enterprises and a few large-scale businesses, however, lack a solid number of small-to-medium enterprises (SMEs) that fuel mass job creation. In reality, this problem often stems from banks having inadequate information about their clients. Credit information is regularly lacking, due in part to an absence of functional credit bureaus. In many cases, the cost of structuring a loan for an SME is also prohibitive, especially considering banks' preference from the outset in working only with larger clients.

Lastly, USG officers should always consider utilization of the Development Credit Authority (DCA) and Global Development Alliance (GDA) when identifying methods to increase funding to entrepreneurs. As of 2010, USAID's DCA portfolio is comprised of 267 guarantees in 64 countries. USAID has made $2.3 billion in private credit available to more than 87,000 borrowers from 191 financial institutions since 1999. Establishment of a DCA loan agreement can bring significant benefits to partner financial institutions and potential borrowers, as well as substantial improvement to the business-enabling environment as a whole, primarily through the ability to reduce the risk of lending (up to 50%) to new sectors and/or new borrowers. DCA programs can be tailored to target specific sectors, with loan sizes typically falling within the range of $5-10 million.

The concept for the GDA started in 2001 and since inception has accounted for 900 alliances and 1,700 distinct partners. The importance of private sector funding cannot be overstated, in that it makes up of more than 80% of investment in developing countries throughout the world. With this in mind, GDAs allow USAID the flexibility to partner with private sector counterparts, NGOs, foreign government bodies, and other organizations, whether it through the provision of cash or in-kind contributions, to leverage resources to expand project impact.

Resource List

Case Studies

- Entrepreneurial Finance Lab: Predicting Entrepreneurial Success
- Grassroots Business Fund (GBF): Strengthening High Impact Businesses"
- Sawari Ventures: Funding the Arab Technology Boom

Key Questions for Program Design

Lessons Learned for Future USG Assistance

Entrepreneurship Development Firm Contact List

- Angel Capital Foundation
- Entrepreneurial Finance Lab
- Grassroots Business Fund
- Sawari Ventures
- Small Enterprise Assistance Fund/Center for Entrepreneurship and Executive Development

USAID Project Summary: Country Guide

- Afghanistan
- Albania
- Armenia
- Azerbaijan
- Bahrain
- Bangladesh
- Belarus
- Bosnia
- Bulgaria
- Cambodia
- Central Asia (region-wide)
- East Africa (region-wide)
- Egypt
- El Salvador
- Georgia
- Global

- Haiti
- Herzegovina
- India
- Indonesia
- Iraq
- Jordan
- Kazakhstan
- Kenya
- Kosovo
- Kuwait
- Kyrgyz Republic
- Kyrgyzstan
- Lebanon
- Liberia
- MENA (region-wide)
- Middle East (region-wide)

- Moldova
- Mongolia
- Morocco
- Oman
- Philippines
- Pakistan
- Paraguay
- Qatar
- Swaziland
- Tajikistan
- Thailand
- Turkey
- Turkmenistan
- United Arab Emirates
- Ukraine
- Uzbekistan

- West Bank/ Gaza
- Yemen
- Zambia
- Zimbabwe

Publications/Reference Materials

Case Studies

Entrepreneurial Finance Lab: Predicting Entrepreneurial Success

The Entrepreneurial Finance Lab (EFL) grew out of the Harvard Center for International Development (CID), after co-founders Bailey Klinger and Asim Khwaja learned of the difficulties faced by entrepreneurs in South Africa to gain access to financing. Following several months of substantial research, they developed a psychometricl tool in 2006-07 aimed at determining the likelihood that an entrepreneur will default on a loan, functioning essentially as a credit score. In generating this figure, the entrepreneur is ranked on a variety of factors, such as intelligence, ethics, and psychological characteristics, which together measure their entrepreneurial ability and their honesty. To test its effectiveness, the co-founders applied this tool to 2,300 entrepreneurs in 7 countries. The results of this study were impressive, in that EFL was "able to meet and exceed the predictive power of credit scoring models in developed countries." Furthermore, they found that "simulated impact on these samples show a reduction in default from 20-45%." A key finding Dr. Klinger notes was that cognitive factors, such as the need for achievement, were much more important indicators of payback than other attributes like risk-taking and optimism.

Entrepreneurial Finance at a Glance

The Entrepreneurial Finance Lab (EFL) grew out of the Harvard Center for International Development (CID). Following several months of substantial research, they developed a psycho-social tool in 2006-07 aimed at determining the likelihood that an entrepreneur will default on a loan; functioning essentially as a credit score. In generating this figure, the entrepreneur is ranked on a variety of factors, such as intelligence, honesty/ethics, and psychological characteristics.

Contact:
Bailey Klinger; info@efinlab.com

The impact of this tool is amplified by the fact that it can be used for assessment of SMEs that do not have available financial statements or history. Generally, it functions best for loan sizes in the range of $1,000-5,000 (intended for micro and small enterprises) and with only slight tweaking can be used remarkably well across geographic regions. However, one area that is problematic is its use when evaluating a company with many directors, since EFL evaluates risk based upon the entrepreneur who runs the company.

EFL was a winner of the G20 SME Finance Challenge for its innovative work in this field and has received assistance from the IFC-administered G20 Innovation Fund, supported in part by USAID. The USG, with expanded financial contribution, could help EFL scale its planned expansion into other countries to realize substantial employment and growth contribution of SMEs. For example, EFL notes, "If the distortion in the firm size distribution in developing countries was removed and the distribution regularized, thus 'filling' the missing middle, estimates suggest GDP across developing countries increasing by over $3.6 trillion dollars annually. This shift would create millions of new SMEs in a handful of our countries of operations alone."

Grassroots Business Fund (GBF): Strengthening High Impact Businesses

The Grassroots Business Fund (GBF) was created within the International Finance Corporation (IFC) in 2004, and in 2008 it became an independent organization. GBF's approach is to provide a blend of investment capital and capacity building to High Impact Businesses in Africa, Asia and Latin America. By targeting for-profit companies that otherwise might fall in the "missing middle," being considered too risky for commercial investment but need much more investment capital than can be provided with microfinance, High Impact Businesses can act as the catalysts for sustainable economic development, employment, and the production of affordable goods and services.

GBF's portfolio consists of equity, quasi-equity, and debt investments. Their average investments are between $500,000 to $1,000,000 over a time period of 5-7 years. In fiscal year 2011 the aggregate value of their portfolio was $8.5 million across 32 businesses. GBF couples their investment capital with technical assistance, ensuring that program managers working on the ground with the local businesses can advise entrepreneurs from start to finish, enabling smart decision-making and investment impact. By the end of 2011, GBF had $2.4 million in technical assistance invested in their businesses.

> *Grassroots Business Fund at a Glance*
>
> Grassroots Business Fund (GBF) was created within the International Finance Corporation (IFC) in 2004 and in 2008 it became an independent organization. They provide investment capital and capacity building to high impact entrepreneurs and SMEs in developing countries. They aim to target the "missing middle" SMEs who will specifically employ or support large numbers of people or have a broader economic range.
>
> Contact:
> Agnes Dasewicz; adasewicz@gbfund.org

Unlike other investment organizations, GBF is unique in that their antecedents in the IFC and broad base of practical experience with other leading players in the industry have helped the organization scaled its efforts and established a solid track record. GBF's model is hands-on, involves intensive staff engagement with portfolio companies, and takes a business-minded approach to improving management, developing business capacities, and expanding its portfolio companies' social and economic impact. In addition, GBF understands that technical assistance is a critical component to helping scale the portfolio company, and they ensure that all investments are carried through with keen advisement.

Agnes Dasewicz, GBF's Chief Operating Officer, lists their three best practices in technical assistance as, "embedding managers, coupling investments with technical assistance, and helping to establish effective corporate boards." Dasewicz explains that once an investment is made, it is important to embed local managers who understand the culture and landscape to "ensure that the investment is allocated properly and that the managers can train others to use the funds wisely." She also notes that through helping firms to grow and establish corporate boards "begins good habits of accountability and transparency." To actualize this, entrepreneurs should "identify people who are experts in what they need advice in and who are objective. Usually they will start out as 'advisors' of colleagues, contacts or business associates, but in the same way boards are formed in the U.S. they can eventually evolve into a more formalized establishment."

GBF believes strongly in collaborating with the USG, viewing them as a partner that has strong resources and recognition. In order to do this, the USG can either work directly with GBF, helping to identify entrepreneurs or businesses that are ripe for investments, or they could directly replicate some of the successes GBF has seen by combining their technical assistance with investment capital. GBF's accomplishment in identifying the appropriate businesses to invest in, in addition to their long-term commitment to advising them throughout the life of the investment, is a crucial component of any entrepreneurship program USAID or the USG would design.

Sawari Ventures: Funding the Arab Technology Boom

Sawari Ventures is an international venture capital firm that primarily funds technology companies in the Middle East and North Africa. They were formalized in 2010 and currently invest in six companies, all in Alexandria and Cairo, Egypt. Some of the companies Sawari is currently investing in include Vimov (http://www.vimov.com/), a consumer technology company whose products include iStimulate and Weather HD, two of the most popular iPhone and iPad apps worldwide. Sawari has also made investments in Kngine (http://www.kngine.com/), a new search engine that provides users with innovative results, personalized answers, and recommendations to their search requests.

> *Sawari Ventures at a Glance*
>
> Sawari Ventures is an international venture capital firm that primarily funds technology companies in the Middle East and North Africa. They were formalized in 2010 and currently invest in six companies, all in Alexandria and Cairo, Egypt.
>
> Contact:
> Leslie Jump; ljump@sawariventures.com

According to Sawari's partner, Leslie Jump, Sawari is in a unique position to excel, given that, "Arab technology companies are growing rapidly and are extremely successful. Much like the U.S. was in the 1990s, there is immense interest in technology companies and start-ups in the Arab world, except now the demand for technology is even stronger." Sawari also sees strong potential in countries like Egypt, even though from an outsider perspective that can be seen as risky. Jump concurs that the investment environment in Egypt post-revolution in January slowed down, but also noticed that "on the entrepreneur side, it [Sawari] has seen much more 'deal flow,' and there is a real sense of empowerment, excitement and willingness to work coming from these entrepreneurs." Sawari is also well-positioned as a firm because technology entrepreneurs have fewer barriers to block them than the traditional entrepreneur. They do not need to worry about how to get their product to market, they usually do not face infrastructure obstacles (such as lack of roads, transportation), and all they need is a small amount of capital and an internet connection.

Sawari recently participated in an Egypt Delegation with GEP shortly before the Egyptian revolution occurred. Sawari identified 11 investors to attend the delegation, many of whom decided immediately during the event to fund a number of entrepreneurs who successfully completed their business plan competition. Many of the investors still are connected to the entrepreneur's months later.

The USG can benefit from future partnerships with Sawari, specifically those working in the MENA region or in the technology sector. Sawari's deep knowledge of the MENA region and the sector categorize them as experts for identifying strong entrepreneur potential and they can easily partner with the USG to fund other talented companies or individuals. Sawari purposely seeks to invest in entrepreneurs with strong promise who will ultimately employ others and have an impact on their countries' overall economy. When looking to connect their beneficiaries to venture capitalists, the USG should seek them out and include them as partners in their events, summits or conferences, or any other opportunities where connecting entrepreneurs to venture capitalists could occur.

Key Questions for Program Design

Budget

- What is the scope of your planned assistance (number of entrepreneurs)?
- Do you have an estimated budget for funding entrepreneurs?
- Will grant funding be incorporated into the program? If yes, how much will be available and how will it be distributed?
- Will matching funds be made available?

Entrepreneur Target Group

- Are there any considerations as to the type of entrepreneurs to fund?
  - Industry-specific
  - Gender
  - First-time entrepreneurs
  - Economically or socially disadvantaged

Potential Investors

- Where will you find potential investors to partner with entrepreneurs?
  - Angel investor groups
  - Venture capital firms
  - Banks/Financial institutions
  - Virtual forums
  - Events (conferences, exhibitions, etc...)
  - Referrals from other organizations

Investment Climate

- Are there any restrictions that will affect funding entrepreneurs?
  - Ownership structure (local vs. foreign)
  - Currency transfer
  - Opening bank accounts
  - Tax implications

Monitoring and Evaluation

- How will you monitor and report on funding entrepreneurs?
  - Number of entrepreneurs funded
  - Value of secured investment
  - Number of investments made

- How will you disaggregate entrepreneurs funded?
  - By age
  - By gender
  - By socio-economic status
  - By geographic location
  - By industry
  - By type
  - By amount

Lessons Learned for Future USG Assistance

1. Venture capital is in most cases not a binding constraint for entrepreneurs. Projects should focus more on facilitation of access to seed and angel funding.

2. Aim to provide targeted funding. The goal should be to connect to sources of finance those who have ideas and the ambition and ability to realize them rather than a generation of entrepreneurs who are responding to the availability of money. In order to actualize targeted funding, aim to identify entrepreneurs who could ultimately employ dozens or hundreds of employees, rather than only a handful. It is these types of entrepreneurs that will eventually fuel economic growth.

3. Access to traditional loans can be accomplished by supporting banks in areas such as structuring and preparing loans for SMEs; providing collateral through funds such as USAID's Development Credit Authority; and supporting the formation of credit bureaus.

4. Developments in virtual platforms, software and psychometric tools represent an excellent opportunity to quickly and effectively identify, assess, and link entrepreneurs to investors and financial institutions throughout the world.

5. Funding the "missing middle" can prove very beneficial. Often times the overstated strengths of microfinance cloud the need for slightly larger amounts of funding; even $10,000-$20,000 could make a huge difference to slightly larger entrepreneurs.

Entrepreneurship Development Firms Contact List

Organization	Contact Name	Email	Website	Focus Area(s)
Angel Capital Foundation (Angel Resource Institute)	Marianne Hudson, Executive Director	mhudson@ angelcapitalassociation. org	www. angelcapitaleducation. org/	Fund *(Primary)* Connect & Sustain *(Secondary)*

Organization Summary
Angel Capital Foundation provides education, training, and information on best practices in the field of angel investing through educational workshops and seminars, research projects and reports. Their target audience includes investors, entrepreneurs, policy makers, and those that support the entrepreneurial ecosystem to build awareness of early-stage capital. While their principal goal is build linkages between angel investors and start-up companies, they also are involved with creating mentoring relationships through their participation in the Startup America Partnership (www.startupamericapartnership.org).

Organization	Contact Name	Email	Website	Focus Area(s)
Entrepreneurial Finance Lab	Bailey Klinger, Director	info@efinlab.com	www.hks.harvard.edu/ centers/cid/programs/ entrepreneurial-finance- lab-research-initiative	Fund *(Primary)* Train *(Secondary)*

Organization Summary

The Entrepreneurial Finance Lab grew out of the Harvard Center for International Development (CID). They have developed a psycho-social tool for determining the likelihood that an entrepreneur will default on a loan, functioning essentially as a credit score. The entrepreneur is ranked on various factors such as intelligence, honesty/ethics, and psychological characteristics. The tool was first developed at CID in 2006-07 and is now conducted by what was spun off and scaled up as a for-profit company. They are currently partnered with Standard Bank in Africa, and have an agreement to launch with BBVA in Mexico in the next two months.

Organization	Contact Name	Email	Website	Focus Area(s)
Grassroots Business Fund (GBF)	Agnes Dasewicz, Chief Operating Officer	adasewicz@gbfund.org	www.gbfund.org	Fund *(Primary)* Train *(Secondary)*

Organization Summary

Grassroots Business Fund provides investments and capacity building to high impact entrepreneurs and SMEs in developing countries. They aim to target "missing middle" SMEs who specifically employ or support large numbers of people or have a broader economic range. They currently work in India, Southeast Asia, Latin America, and Africa.

Organization	Contact Name	Email	Website	Focus Area(s)
Sawari Ventures	Leslie Jump, Partner	ljump@sawariventures. com	www.sawariventures. com/	Fund *(Primary)*

Organization Summary

Sawari Ventures is a venture capital firm that primarily funds technology companies in the Middle East and North Africa. They were formalized in 2010, and currently invest in six companies, all in Egypt. Sawari Ventures focuses on technology, because similar to the United States in the 1990's, it is an emerging industry, except there is even more demand for technology today. Technology is also low cost and extremely fast – for example, mobile apps take only a few days to develop and are very low cost for the entrepreneurs, so venture capital funding stretches far.

Organization	Contact Name	Email	Website	Focus Area(s)
Small Enterprise Assistance Funds (SEAF) / Center for Entrepreneurship and Executive Development (CEED)	Tom Drum, Vice President of Global Business Development (SEAF) Peter Righi, Global Director (CEED)	tom@seafweb.org (SEAF) PRighi@seafweb.org (CEED)	www.seaf.com www.ceed-global.org/	Fund *(Primary)* Train; Connect & Sustain *(Secondary)*

Organization Summary

The Small Enterprise Assistance Fund (SEAF) is an investment management organization that provides capital and business assistance to SME's worldwide. SEAF focuses on growth-oriented SME's in emerging markets, or the "missing middle," those firms in need of $25,000- $250,000 in investment. SEAF believes that by investing in such companies, real growth can evolve.

The Center for Entrepreneurship and Executive Development (CEED) is a USAID-developed and funded project, utilizing reflows from SEAF's various venture capital investment funds, to provide entrepreneurs and their respective executive teams with the knowledge, skills, and networks needed to accelerate their businesses. CEED has active centers operating in Southeast Europe (Bulgaria, Macedonia, Romania, and Slovenia) and plans to expand to Bangladesh and other Asian countries as a springboard for future Global Engagement activities in the Middle East.

CEED assists entrepreneurs by offering training, consulting, and business networking services in three areas: entrepreneurial growth, access to finance, and developing new markets. Of particular note, CEED operates "Top Class," a one-year program aimed at helping young entrepreneurs develop the skills they need to grow operations. The program combines monthly training in leadership, marketing, and financial management, as well as a mentorship program that gives budding entrepreneurs access to veteran business leaders. CEED is a well-recognized initiative, earning accolades from current Prime Minister Vladimir Putin as a major contributor to SME development in Russia and received a Distinguished Service Group Award from USAID for its innovative approach to promoting entrepreneurship.

Back to Top - Fund   *Back to Resource List – Fund*

Enable

Best Practices

The most striking facet regarding the business enabling environment is that while most organizations interviewed believe this is an important and necessary area for assistance, few are actively involved in implementing such activities. The main reason for this appears to be related to the length of time needed to effect real change, with many respondents noting an expected minimum of at least 10 years. Additionally, macro-level improvement often demands advocacy from representatives of the highest-levels of government to which many organizations simply do not have access, compounded by the fact that personnel in these positions "turn over" often, forcing organizations to start relationship-building from scratch.

Another interesting outcome of our research and interviews relates to the perceived impact of bureaucratic hurdles, such as those measured by the <u>Doing Business</u> Index, which many entrepreneurs feel is overstated. This is not to say that the conduciveness of a country's legal and regulatory environment does not directly affect the ability for an entrepreneur to operate, but instead highlights that improvement of the business enabling environment is not the "silver bullet" that it may often be portrayed as being. For example, while starting a business can be challenging and many times doing so is legally is extraordinarily difficult, enterprising entrepreneurs generally a find a way around obstacles to achieve their objectives.

There was one very notable exception, in that while these hurdles were typically not considered insurmountable by formal enterprises, they do have a significant bearing on the decisions of informal enterprises about whether and when to register (formalize). While perhaps most informal enterprises are actually necessity-based entrepreneurs who have little intention of growing and may in some cases have a vested interest in "staying under the radar" to avoid being noticed either by the tax authorities or by larger enterprises, those that have growth aspirations may be discouraged from joining the formal sector by the presence of unreasonably long waiting periods or exorbitantly high costs associated with obtaining the permits necessary to open a business. Similarly, the high cost, length of time, and labor constraints associated with closing a business can also be problematic.

Although enabling improvement obstacles are formidable, BGI, through its interviews, found that the USG is regarded as the most as the most suitable body to undertake activities in this sphere. Interviewees noted this is a combination of the USG's on-going access to the top echelons of government, its long-term perspective towards development (especially with regard to macro-level economic progress), and is in close alignment with promoting American trade policy. Business-enabling environment projects should continue to be implemented (e.g., USAID) and expanded upon as possible to achieve more holistic improvements. Examples of assistance include: encouraging changes to a nation's corporate tax code to make opening and operating a business more conducive to entrepreneurs; reducing barriers to trade and investment to increase the influx of capital; and reducing cumbersome legislation which creates market inefficiencies.

Resource List

Case Studies

- Council on Competitiveness: Setting an Action Agenda

Key Questions for Program Design

Lessons Learned for Future USG Assistance

Entrepreneurship Development Firm Contact List

- American Chamber of Commerce Egypt
- Council on Competitiveness

USAID Project Summary: Country Guide

• Afghanistan	• Haiti	• Moldova	• West Bank/
• Albania	• Herzegovina	• Mongolia	Gaza
• Armenia	• India	• Morocco	• Yemen
• Azerbaijan	• Indonesia	• Oman	• Zambia
• Bahrain	• Iraq	• Philippines	• Zimbabwe
• Bangladesh	• Jordan	• Pakistan	
• Belarus	• Kazakhstan	• Paraguay	
• Bosnia	• Kenya	• Qatar	
• Bulgaria	• Kosovo	• Swaziland	
• Cambodia	• Kuwait	• Tajikistan	
• Central Asia (region-wide)	• Kyrgyz Republic	• Thailand	
• East Africa (region-wide)	• Kyrgyzstan	• Turkey	
• Egypt	• Lebanon	• Turkmenistan	
• El Salvador	• Liberia	• United Arab Emirates	
• Georgia	• MENA (region-wide)	• Ukraine	
• Global	• Middle East (region-wide)	• Uzbekistan	

Publications/Reference Materials

Council on Competitiveness: Setting an Action Agenda

The Council on Competitiveness is comprised of 175 national leaders whose mission is to "set an action agenda that drives U.S. economic competitiveness and results in a rising standard of living for American citizens." Since 1986, the Council has continued to hold member conferences to develop strategies, requisite actions, and publish policy and concept papers to guide the debate concerning America's long-term competitiveness position. The Council is actively involved in helping American investors and businesses operate in foreign markets, while at the same time providing assistance to foreign-owned companies interested in establishing a presence in the United States. This two-fold strategic approach is in alignment with globalization, in that the U.S. is only one of many extremely competitive players in the world market; however, their approach is tailored to ensure American interests are at the forefront of the USG's strategic decision making.

The Council on Competitiveness at a Glance

The Council on Competitiveness is comprised of 175 national leaders whose mission is to "set an action agenda that drives U.S. economic competitiveness and results in a rising standard of living for American citizens." Since 1986, the Council has continued to hold member conferences to develop strategies, requisite actions, and publish policy and concept papers to guide the debate concerning America's long-term competitiveness position.

Contact:
Chad Evans; cevans@compete.org

In its efforts, the Council typically focuses on creating a favorable economic infrastructure in foreign markets that will increase the flow of investment and result in job creation. The USG has an obvious ally in the Council on Competitiveness in that it is in its inherent interest to promote American interests abroad. When designing entrepreneurship programs, the USG can utilize the Council's world-class metrics on how to evaluate competitiveness and could tap into its membership base to potentially serve as mentors and, as applicable, create investment linkages to foreign entrepreneurs. This is especially true for more high-impact entrepreneurs who have the potential to scale and are interested in establishing a more formal relationship with American businesses, either in their home country or in the United States.

Key Questions for Program Design

Budget

- What is the scope of your planned assistance (impact on the business enabling environment?)

- Do you have an estimated budget for enabling entrepreneurs?

Business Environment

- Do you have adequate buy-in and support from key local counterparts to make changes to the enabling environment?

  - National level

  - Regional level

  - Local level

- Is there a historical framework for change/improvement to the business enabling environment?

- Which areas will most likely be impacted by the planned changes to be made?

  - Business registration

  - Business licensing

  - Tax codes

  - Trade (import/export)

  - Investment regulations

  - Ownership/Incorporation legislation

Entrepreneur Target Group

- How will entrepreneurs be most affected by the proposed changes?

- What are the key objectives associated with improving the business enabling environment?

Monitoring and Evaluation

- How will you monitor and report on enabling entrepreneurs?

  - Number of laws and policies eliminated/amended beneficial to entrepreneurs

  - Value of laws and policies eliminated/amended beneficial to entrepreneurs

  - Number of entrepreneurs impacted

  - Type of entrepreneurs impacted

Lessons Learned for Future USG Assistance

1. Reducing bureaucracy is a particularly important component of reducing the cost of business operations and risk associated with investment, and in encouraging informal entrepreneurs to formally register. However, reducing bureaucracy seems to matter less to formal entrepreneurs. Set reasonable expectations for the impact on entrepreneurship of interventions designed to assist countries in this area.

2. Initiatives designed to lower bureaucratic obstacles in order to encourage registration of informal entrepreneurs should be accompanied by an information campaign designed to make such entrepreneurs aware of the changes.

3. For growth entrepreneurs, policy changes, in other less obvious areas may have an equal or greater impact. For example, stronger anti-monopoly policy will increase the number of perceived opportunities and can lead to greater entrepreneurial activity.

Entrepreneurship Development Firms Contact List

Organization	Contact Name	Email	Website	Focus Area(s)
American Chamber of Commerce (Egypt)	Hashim Fahmy, Chief Executive Officer	hfahmy@amcham.org.eg	www.amcham.org.eg	Enable *(Primary)* Connect & Sustain ; Train *(Secondary)*

Organization Summary

The American Chamber of Commerce Egypt (AmCham Egypt) views itself primarily as an enabler to support entrepreneurs. It achieves this by serving as a platform for forums, public events, and delegations which gives prominent local and U.S. business leaders the opportunity to raise issues to solicit government action. In addition, AmCham Egypt also provides member companies and non-member individual access to training at their Career Development Center (CDC), and also promotes linkages to trade through its Business Matchmaking online service, and publications, and through hosting over 170 special events each year.

Council on Competitiveness	Chad Evans, Senior Vice President	cevans@compete.org	www.compete.org	Enable *(Primary)*

Organization Summary

The Council on Competitiveness is comprised of 175 national leaders whose mission is to "set an action agenda that drives U.S. economic competitiveness and results in a rising standard of living for American citizens." Since 1986, the Council has continued to hold member conferences to develop strategies, requisite actions, and publish policy and concept papers to guide the debate concerning America's long-term competitiveness position.

Back to Top - Enable   *Back to Resource List – Enable*

Celebrate

Best Practices

A major reason why entrepreneurship is stifled in a number of developing countries is because culturally it is simply not accepted. Many entrepreneurs will fail multiple times before they succeed, and the idea of failing can lead to shame or disapproval by family members, friends, and peers. Promoting the idea that entrepreneurship is a viable path to success and celebrating one's own ambitions and ideas is crucial to ultimately stimulating growth. Increasing the visibility of entrepreneurs' successes is an important tool towards reinforcing the role they play in society and increases the likelihood that others will become interested in following suit. Most commonly, events that fulfill this objective are likely part of a larger venue, and as such bring high visibility. Examples of this include the recognition of business plan competition finalists during GEP's Egypt Delegation or the selection of the "Young Entrepreneur of the Year" as done by INJAZ al-Arab during their annual entrepreneurship conference. While many such examples are competition-based, another well-represented method, especially for virtual platforms, is use of entrepreneur "success stories." This medium is particularly effective in concisely "telling the story" of an entrepreneur, typically summarizing the challenges he or she faced in eventually attaining success. It also provides others with a sense of connection, in that they may share a background or experiences similar to that of the showcased entrepreneur.

Those who were interviewed regarding maximizing the impact of celebrating entrepreneurs cited relevance (meaning the public's ability to understand and appreciate his or her contribution) to others as an important factor. This is especially important in societies whose collective perception of entrepreneurs and entrepreneurship may be dampened. To ensure this happens, host organizations most often select those native to the country/region where the celebratory event is taking place; however, choice can be tailored even further to include entrepreneurs from the same the same industry or sector as that of the audience. It should not be surprising that it is often easier to evaluate individuals or situations using one's own cultural context, which is a valuable point to consider when organizing celebratory events. Additionally, utilization of this model facilitates a greater sense of transference to occur between the entrepreneur and the public at large, reinforcing an increased sense of possibility among attendees, well-illustrated in the saying that, "If he/she can do it, I can do it."

Resource List

Case Studies

- Entrepreneur's Organization: Global Student Entrepreneur Awards
- Global Entrepreneurship Week: A Celebration of Success

Key Questions for Program Design

Lessons Learned for Future USG Assistance

Entrepreneurship Development Firm Contact List

- Entrepreneurs' Organization
- Global Entrepreneurship Week
- Google Indonesia

USAID Project Summary: Country Guide

• Afghanistan	• Haiti	• Moldova	• West Bank/
• Albania	• Herzegovina	• Mongolia	Gaza
• Armenia	• India	• Morocco	• Yemen
• Azerbaijan	• Indonesia	• Oman	• Zambia
• Bahrain	• Iraq	• Philippines	• Zimbabwe
• Bangladesh	• Jordan	• Pakistan	
• Belarus	• Kazakhstan	• Paraguay	
• Bosnia	• Kenya	• Qatar	
• Bulgaria	• Kosovo	• Swaziland	
• Cambodia	• Kuwait	• Tajikistan	
• Central Asia (region-wide)	• Kyrgyz Republic	• Thailand	
• East Africa (region-wide)	• Kyrgyzstan	• Turkey	
• Egypt	• Lebanon	• Turkmenistan	
• El Salvador	• Liberia	• United Arab Emirates	
• Georgia	• MENA (region-wide)	• Ukraine	
• Global	• Middle East (region-wide)	• Uzbekistan	

Publications/Reference Materials

Case Studies

Entrepreneurs' Organization: Global Student Entrepreneur Awards

The Global Student Entrepreneur Awards (GSEA) is one of the key programs offered by The Entrepreneurs' Organization (EO), an international network of over 7,500 members from over 38 countries, whose vision is "to build the world's most influential community of entrepreneurs through peer-to-peer connectivity to enable entrepreneurs to learn and grow."

GSEA is held on an annual basis during Global Entrepreneurship Week and includes student finalists from all over the world. The purpose of this program is to both inspire and create visibility for student entrepreneurs who run innovative and socially responsible enterprises. The program is open to enrolled high school, undergraduate and graduate students who at a minimum have owned and operated a for-profit business for the last six consecutive months. Once nominated, participants compete in local, regional and/or virtual competitions, in which one finalist is selected as the high school, undergraduate, or graduate student award recipient.

Global Student Entrepreneur Awards at a Glance

The Global Student Entrepreneur Awards (GSEA) is one of the key programs offered by The Entrepreneurs' Organization (EO), an international network of over 7,500 members from over 38 countries, whose vision is "to build the world's most influential community of entrepreneurs through peer-to-peer connectivity to enable entrepreneurs to learn and grow."

Contact:
Kevin Langley/Adrienne Cornelson/ Bob Strade; klangley@eonetwork.org; acornelsen@insite.net; bstrade@eonetwork.org

Finalists in each category receive a $10,000 cash prize, as well as access to tens of thousands of dollars in business services and products provided by EO members. In addition to financial compensation, competitors gain a distinct advantage by expanding their professional business network, meeting other student entrepreneurs and supporters from the business community, gaining valuable feedback about their business plans, and receiving increased visibility through media exposure.

The USG could become involved in this event, either as a sponsor or by serving as a judge throughout the competition process. Furthermore, it should examine ways in which it could link competitors to other entrepreneurship programs, particularly when hosting events to celebrate entrepreneurial success.

Global Entrepreneurship Week (GEW): A Celebration of Success

Global Entrepreneurship Week is the world's largest celebration of the innovators and job creators, who launch startups that bring ideas to life, drive economic growth and expand human welfare. It is also a great way for partners to promote and shape an entrepreneurial culture in the communities and countries around them.

During one week each November, GEW inspires people everywhere through local, national and global activities designed to help them explore their potential as self-starters and innovators. These activities, from large-scale competitions and events to intimate networking gatherings, connect participants to potential collaborators, mentors and even investors—introducing them to new possibilities and exciting opportunities.

The initiative kicked off in 2008, launched by former UK Prime Minister Gordon Brown and Carl Schramm, the president and CEO of the Ewing Marion Kauffman Foundation. Since then, it has grown to 119 countries—with nearly 24,000 partner organizations planning more than 37,000 activities that directly engage more than 7 million people.

Grassroots Business Fund at a Glance

Global Entrepreneurship Week (GEW) is the world's largest celebration of entrepreneurship, connecting millions of people worldwide and encouraging them to participate and host events focusing on entrepreneurship during the same week each year.

Contact:
Brenden Chaney;
bmchaney@unleashingideas.org

With so many new jobs in entrepreneurial economies coming from firms less than five years old, it is not surprising that leaders around the world are looking to reinvigorate their economies by focusing on ways to stimulate new firm formation. Global Entrepreneurship Week helps map the entrepreneurial ecosystem in those countries and enjoys the participation and support of presidents and prime ministers on every continent. But GEW is more than just an awareness campaign supported by world leaders and celebrity entrepreneurs. It is about unleashing ideas and doing what it takes to bring them to life—spotting opportunities, taking risks, solving problems, being creative, building connections and learning from both failure and success.

According to Brenden Chaney at GEW, "The best marketing is word of mouth"—spreading the word from country to country to inspire others to lead their national campaign or simply host an event. Chaney also recommends that partners overseas such as U.S. Embassies or USAID Missions "identify a smaller network of strategic partners and champions. Smaller organizations can often be the most excited and can initiate grassroots movements. Big names help, but smaller ones can develop big impacts over time."

In order to host a GEW activity, all one needs to do contact them directly (via the GEW website) to register their event. As long as the event supports, promotes, or discusses entrepreneurship, it can be included. If a USAID Mission or Embassy is interested in hosting an event but doesn't have any concrete ideas, GEW can provide insight into what has worked well in other locations. Alternatively, GEW can be leveraged to identify local partners already existing in their areas with whom they can partner to hold a local event. GEW's plethora of contacts in a variety of organizations, universities and individuals can always be connected to local government resources for event coordination.

The unique, fluid and open nature of GEW makes it an organization with which it is easy and simple for USAID or Embassies to work. While many USAID Missions or Embassies already work directly with GEW, there are a number that have not and might find it very easy to do so. An event can be as simple as a roundtable discussion, a networking event, small conference, or gathering of entrepreneurs, business owners, implementers, academics, or government officials to discuss entrepreneurship. BGI would recommend that any partners take advantage of this straightforward opportunity to promote and celebrate the culture of entrepreneurship with GEW.

Key Questions for Program Design

Budget
- What is the scope of your planned assistance (number of entrepreneurs/events)?
- Do you have an estimated amount budgeted for celebrating entrepreneurs? If yes, how much?
- Have you established per unit costs for conducting celebratory events? If yes, how much?

Entrepreneur Target Group
- Where will you find entrepreneurs to celebrate?
  - Educational institutions (colleges, universities, technical schools, etc...)
  - Professional associations
  - Virtual forums
  - Trainings
  - Events (conferences, exhibitions, etc...)
  - Referrals from other organizations

Celebration Format
- What type of format will you use to celebrate entrepreneurs?
  - Business plan competitions
  - Entrepreneurship award ceremonies
  - Large-scale venues (conferences, exhibitions)
  - Tie-in to private sector business events
  - Virtual (websites, social media forums, email distribution lists)

Communications
- How will you broadcast celebratory events?
  - Websites
  - Newspaper
  - Radio
  - Television
  - Referrals
  - Word-of-Mouth
- Do you have estimated costs for the applicable mediums?

Monitoring and Evaluation
- How will you monitor and report on the celebration of entrepreneurs?
  - Number of entrepreneurs celebrated
  - Number of events held
  - Number of people reached through broadcast mediums

- How will you disaggregate entrepreneurs celebrated?
  - By age
  - By gender
  - By socio-economic status
  - By geographic location
  - By industry
  - By celebration format

Lessons Learned for Future USG Assistance

1. Celebrating success is an important contributor to mindset change and can be effectively done through media events, highly publicized awards, and government literature, speeches, and interviews.

2. Showcasing entrepreneurs may best occur as part of highly attended conferences and conventions to generate a "stir" among the audience and ensure ample visibility for the entrepreneur.

3. Word-of-mouth promotion is often the most effective yet least expensive tool for proselytizing entrepreneurs and entrepreneurship as a field.

4. Tailor the choice of entrepreneurs or successes to highlight in accordance with the profile of the audience. Remember that local (native) examples are more powerful and relevant to an audience.

5. Do not forget to include smaller organizations both as examples to showcase and as invitees. While "big names" may generate interest, the enthusiasm and excitement of smaller firms may easily spread to a large segment of the entrepreneurial population.

Entrepreneurship Development Firms Contact List

Organization	Contact Name	Email	Website	Focus Area(s)
Entrepreneurs' Organization (EO)	Bob Strade, Executive Director; Kevin Langley, Global Chairman; Adrienne Cornelsen, 2011-2012 Global Communications Chair	bstrade@eonetwork.org ; klangley@eonetwork.org ; acornelsen@eonetwork.org	www.eonetwork.org	Connect & Sustain *(Primary)* Celebrate *(Secondary)*

Organization Summary

The Entrepreneurs' Organization (EO) is a dynamic, global network of more than 8,000 business owners in 40 countries, whose mission is to enable entrepreneurs to learn and grow from each other, leading to greater business success and an enriched personal life. EO operates the Global Student Entrepreneur Awards program to recognize outstanding undergraduate students running a business and its Accelerator Program, which is the catalyst that enables first-stage entrepreneurs to catapult their business to the next level. The mission of the program is to empower these entrepreneurs with the tools they need to grow their businesses to more than more than $ 1 million in sales, and provide them with the skills to make them better entrepreneurs and leaders. Along with structured educational content focused on the core area of first-stage businesses, the Accelerator Program affords the unique experience of learning from and connecting with the world's most influential entrepreneurs.

Organization	Contact Name	Email	Website	Focus Area(s)
Global Entrepreneurship Week (GEW)	Brenden Chaney	bmchaney@ unleashingideas.org	www.gew.org.uk	Celebrate *(Primary)* Connect & Sustain *(Secondary)*

Organization Summary

Global Entrepreneurship Week (GEW) started in the UK through Enterprise Week with Gordon Brown and Jonathan Ortmans from the Kauffmann foundation. Through that, Global Entrepreneurship America began and in one year expanded internationally. The first GEW was held in 2008, and has since expanded into 115 countries. The last GEW had more than seven million participants and 24,000 partners. Its overall mission is to build an entrepreneurship awareness campaign and to inspire anyone to become an entrepreneur.

Organization	Contact Name	Email	Website	Focus Area(s)
Google, Indonesia	Ishi Singh, New Business Development Director	ishi@google.com	www.google.com/about/ corporate/company	Celebrate *(Primary)* Connect & Sustain *(Secondary)*

Organization Summary

Google, Inc. is focused on improving the ways people connect with information. To encourage business development, Google sponsors a business competition and provides funds for awards. They encourage application writers to use Google platforms to host their software, and provide free start-up for App writers. In addition, Google provides technical expertise and mentors their partner entrepreneurs.

Back to Top - Celebrate   *Back to Resource List – Celebrate*

Mixed Models

Best Practices

Although the cases presented above highlight a particular aspect that stands out about these organizations' work, many of the organizations we examined pursue what may be referred to as "mixed models" for supporting entrepreneurship (i.e., they cover two or more of the six pillars of entreprneurship). A common theme garnered from many of the individuals with whom we spoke was that it is critical to get all aspects of the entrepreneurial ecosystem aligned. Even, as it became clear that certain elements are perhaps underappreciated (mindset, entrepreneurship education), while the importance of others has been overstated (donor-supported incubators, legal and regulatory environment), failure to get any one element right can cause the entire system to function at a sub-optimal level. This is also true at the entrepreneur level, in that training without funding and connections does not generally produce the desired results, while at the same time, funding without the accompanying training also falls short of the desired effect. Similarly, incubators that provide infrastructure alone have proven to be less effective than those that provide a full system of support. While this does not necessarily imply that all organizations must work across all elements of the system, organizations that do can offer entrepreneurial communities a unique, cross-disciplinary approach.

Resource List

Case Studies

- CMEA Capital: A Step Beyond Funding
- Commitment to Capacity Building & Economic Empowerment
    - Goldman Sachs *10,000 Women*
    - Citi Foundation
- Oasis 500: A Wealth of Resources
- Queen Rania Center for Entrepreneurship: "Made in Jordan" Entrepreneurship

Key Questions for Program Design

Lessons Learned for Future USG Assistance

Entrepreneurship Development Firm Contact List

- Citi Foundation
- CMEA Capital
- Goldman Sachs 10,000 Women
- Oasis 500
- Queen Rania Center for Entrepreneurship

USAID Project Summary: Country Guide

- Afghanistan
- Albania
- Armenia
- Azerbaijan
- Bahrain
- Bangladesh
- Belarus
- Bosnia
- Bulgaria
- Cambodia
- Central Asia (region-wide)
- East Africa (region-wide)
- Egypt
- El Salvador
- Georgia
- Global

- Haiti
- Herzegovina
- India
- Indonesia
- Iraq
- Jordan
- Kazakhstan
- Kenya
- Kosovo
- Kuwait
- Kyrgyz Republic
- Kyrgyzstan
- Lebanon
- Liberia
- MENA (region-wide)
- Middle East (region-wide)

- Moldova
- Mongolia
- Morocco
- Oman
- Philippines
- Pakistan
- Paraguay
- Qatar
- Swaziland
- Tajikistan
- Thailand
- Turkey
- Turkmenistan
- United Arab Emirates
- Ukraine
- Uzbekistan

- West Bank/ Gaza
- Yemen
- Zambia
- Zimbabwe

Publications/Reference Materials

Case Studies

CMEA Capital: A Step Beyond Funding

CMEA Capital is a venture capital firm based in San Francisco that invests in entrepreneurs and companies focused in the energy (alternative energies), information technology (software, semiconductors and emerging internet technologies), and life sciences (drug development, medical device and diagnostics companies) sectors. Investments range from $0.5 million to $50 million and are made to individuals and companies across the business spectrum, from first-time novices to serial entrepreneurs. CMEA Capital's efforts center around fostering scientific advancement, due to the enormous impact it could have on people throughout the world. CMEA Capital's two core principles are "an unshakeable faith in the opportunities of scientific discovery" and "its ability to identify those opportunities and bring them to market."

CMEA Capital at a Glance

CMEA Capital is a venture capital firm based in San Francisco that invests in entrepreneurs and companies focused in the energy (alternative energies), information technology (software, semiconductors and emerging internet technologies), and life sciences (drug development, medical device and diagnostics companies) sectors.

Contact:
Faysal Sohail; faysal@cmea.com

A key feature inherent in its operations is the belief that successful entrepreneurs require more than just ideas and capital. Thus, in addition to finding sources of funding, CMEA Capital provides entrepreneurs the opportunity to form relationships with a network of corporate partners. In particular, this network is comprised of individuals who have succeeded in the same the sectors as that of the target entrepreneur. Corporate partners serve as guides and advisors, sharing their experiences with partner entrepreneurs on a wide range of topics, from the technical aspects connected to their products to the processes behind growing a business in their particular field. In addition, the respective successes of these corporate sponsors serve to encourage and motivate entrepreneurs and provides them with the opportunity to learn how to avoid costly mistakes.

By taking a combined approach to assisting entrepreneurs through connections to both funding sources and mentors, CMEA Capital believes it greatly improves an entrepreneur's chance of long-term success. The company could be part of a more systematic mechanism to connect entrepreneurs in developing countries with investors in Silicon Valley. Although corporate partners could be based in the U.S., they could also originate in the country of the entrepreneur. By doing so, the mentorship would be adapted, not only to the particular sector of activity of that entrepreneur, but also to the specific context in which he or she operates. The USG, through its presence and network of contacts in countries throughout the world, could help in facilitating this type of mentorship exchange program.

Commitment to Capacity Building & Economic Empowerment

Goldman Sachs *10,000 Women*

10,000 Women is a five-year investment by Goldman Sachs to provide underserved female entrepreneurs around the world with a business and management education. Research conducted by Goldman Sachs and the World Bank over several years has shown that investing in education for women has a significant multiplier effect, leading to more productive workers, healthier and better-educated families, and ultimately to more prosperous communities. The program operates through a network of more than 75 academic and nonprofit institutions. These partnerships help develop locally relevant coursework and improve the quality and capacity of business education worldwide. The women selected for the program enroll in customized certification programs ranging in duration from five weeks to six months. Topics covered include marketing, accounting, writing business plans and accessing capital. Students are offered mentoring and post-graduate support by partner institutions, local businesses and the people of Goldman Sachs. Funding for *10,000 Women* is provided by Goldman Sachs and the Goldman Sachs Foundation.

10,000 Women at a Glance

10,000 Women is a five-year investment by Goldman Sachs to provide underserved female entrepreneurs around the world with a business and management education. Research has shown that investing in education in women leads to more productive workers, healthier and better-educated families, and ultimately to more prosperous communities.

Contact:
Noa Myer; noa.meyer@gs.com

Citi Foundation

Under a successful partnership launched in 2006, Citigroup business and the Overseas Private Investment Corporation (OPIC) have provided more than $266 million in funding to 30 microfinance institutions (MFIs) across 17 countries. The MFIs have created microloans for more than 900,000 borrowers, 92% of whom are women. Citi Foundation, the corporate foundation of Citigroup, funds projects in 86 countries where Citigroup operates and awarded $68 million in 2010 for development projects. Examples of its assistance efforts include grants for the Egyptian Economic Empowerment of Women Project (www.eacdonline.com) and the Junior Achievement Turkey-Young Enterprise Europe program (www.young-enterprise.org). Citi Foundation supports the economic empowerment and financial inclusion of low-to moderate-income people in communities where Citi operates. For example, since 2005, Citi Foundation has invested almost $10 million to support entrepreneurs in 28 countries over 5 continents through the Citi Microentrepreneurship Awards Program. By working with leading microfinance institutions, monetary awards are provided to entrepreneurs as further financial backing to those who have borrowed as little as $12 and transformed a life of poverty into a life of possibility.

Citi Foundation at a Glance

Citi Foundation, the corporate foundation of Citigroup, funds projects in 86 countries where Citigroup operates and last year gave away more than $68 million for development projects. They work with local partners to implement these projects, which primarily focus on financial capability and asset building, microfinance, enterprise development, college success (in the U.S.), youth education and livelihoods (globally), and neighborhood revitalization (in the U.S.).

Contact:
Irena Shiba; Shibai@citi.com

In order to implement its programs, Citi Foundation works collaboratively with a range of local partners to design and test financial inclusion innovations with potential to achieve scale and support leadership and knowledge building activities. Citi Foundation utilizes a results-oriented measurement framework to assess the impact of the programs it funds. Every investment is carefully tracked to identify ways to ensure success and understand what works and why. This framework helps to define more clearly the results sought from investments in each of its core focus areas, which include: financial capability and asset building; microfinance; enterprise development; college success (in the U.S.); youth education and livelihoods (globally); and neighborhood revitalization (in the U.S.). In each of its core priorities, Citi Foundation partners with organizations that demonstrate a commitment to sustainability and incorporate sound environmental practices in its programs.

While both Goldman Sachs and Citi Foundation partner primarily with local NGOs, non-profits, universities, and practitioners to implement these projects, there is a unique opportunity for the USG to leverage them in order to establish public-private partnerships. Both firms are in exclusive positions because they have already established worldwide brand recognition through their general business operations. But as Graham Macmillan of Citi Foundations duly notes, "Working with the U.S. Government amplifies what we do." Both firms expressed agreement in the strength they see that the USG has when establishing strong policy objectives overseas, and they are interested in working with the USG, especially through workshops, conferences, or high-level events to promote a positive culture of entrepreneurship. Both firms have established names, resources, and connections that can be paired with USG resources to connect and network government officials, policy makers and leaders for knowledge-sharing, promoting sound policies, and demonstrating unity at the public-private level that can have deep ripple effects throughout entrepreneurship programs.

Oasis 500: A Wealth of Resources

Oasis 500 is a for-profit investment company that aims at accelerating the development of entrepreneurs in Jordan and the MENA region. Its accelerator model focuses on companies in the fields of ICT, digital media and mobile. Oasis 500 provides multiple opportunities to entrepreneurs, including boot camp training, equity financing, and links to mentors and investors. Oasis 500's model starts with an open invitation (typically through radio stations and events, although word-of-mouth is now increasingly prevalent) for to entrepreneurs to submit a concept briefing. Following an interview, those entrepreneurs selected as having the best ideas (60 are brought in every six weeks) are offered a 6 day intensive boot camp training in topics such as, how to start a business, finance, marketing of technology products, and pitching to investors, all funded by company sponsorships which require future use of their services.

> **Oasis 500 at a Glance**
>
> Oasis 500 is a for profit investment company, focused on developing entrepreneurs in Jordan and the MENA region, working in the fields of ICT, digital media and mobile. It offers multiple services to entrepreneurs, including boot camp training, equity financing, and links to investors.
>
> **Contact:**
> Salwa Katkhuda; Salwa@oasis500.com

From this group, only about 10% are selected by Oasis 500 to receive $15,000 and 3 months of incubation services and mentoring from a network of 150 business professionals, in exchange for a 10% equity stake in their enterprise. Each entrepreneur is preliminarily matched with four potential mentors and through an in-person "meet and greet" event, entrepreneurs and mentors attempt to identify a mutual fit. Mentors are generally motivated solely by personal satisfaction, but for some the opportunity to take equity in these companies early on is also an incentive.

For the top entrepreneurs from this group, Oasis 500 offers another round of investment, if deemed necessary. Oasis 500 connects those that are ready to "take flight" on their own to a network of nearly 100 angel investors from the first regional Angel Network that they operate. Since September 2010, Oasis 500 has trained 200 enterprises and provided funding to 25 of them. The name refers to the organization's target of funding 500 enterprises in 5 years in Jordan and beyond.

It would behoove the USG to more fully examine organizations, such as Oasis 500, which exemplify a more comprehensive approach to entrepreneurship assistance. As shown above, the USG could use a mixed-model that incorporates not only the elements illustrated above, from identification to funding, but also offers both assistance in improving the business environment ("enable entrepreneurs") and opportunities to promote the success of entrepreneurs ("celebrate entrepreneurs").

Queen Rania Center for Entrepreneurship: "Made In Jordan" Entrepreneurship

The Queen Rania Center for Entrepreneurship, based in Amman, Jordan, was established in 2004 as a non-profit organization to support technology-based entrepreneurs in the country, in industry sectors such as ICT, clean technology (food, water, and energy), biotech/ life sciences, as well as security and defense. The Center's focus is on the 3-4% of entrepreneurs who are considered true "growth entrepreneurs" interested in growing their enterprises.

The Center began as an initiative to raise awareness by supporting a cultural shift in attitude favoring entrepreneurship. The Center is currently moving into its second phase, which includes the development of programs to support startups, and it hopes to ultimately develop into a regional Center of Excellence capable of delivering services to entrepreneurship initiatives outside of Jordan. The Center now offers four key programs: the Queen Rania National Entrepreneurship Competition; an Industry-University Linkages Competition; Entrepreneurship University Clubs (DART); and Global Entrepreneurship Week.

> ### Queen Rania Center at a Glance
>
> The Queen Rania Center for Entrepreneurship is a non-profit organization to support technology-based, "growth" entrepreneurs in Jordan to expand their enterprises.
>
> Contact: Farhan Kaladeh; http://www.qrce. org/?q=contact

The National Entrepreneurship Competition is designed to foster entrepreneurial spirit, develop the entrepreneurial skills of participants, and create awareness around potential opportunities in technology. The competition features three tracks: a universities track (which includes both students and faculty members, and which constitutes the majority of participants); a pre-startup track for entrepreneurs at the "idea" stage who lack a business plan; and a startup track, in which a basic business plan exists and there is some evidence of commercial activity. For the competition's winners, the Center runs a "Boot Camp" that includes business training and mentoring.

The Industry-University Linkages program, known as "Made in Jordan," is designed to recognize outstanding R&D projects and showcase success stories, while also developing the skills of participants and reinforcing university-industry linkages. Through the program, students and faculty from universities are charged with addressing private sector problems. Winners benefit from both recognition and cash prizes. University Entrepreneurship Clubs (i.e. the DART program, an acronym for Dream, Aim, Reach, Target) encourage students to explore entrepreneurship as a career path. Finally, Global Entrepreneurship Week, sponsored by the Kauffman Foundation, provides an opportunity to showcase and celebrate Jordanian entrepreneurs.

The Queen Rania Center for Entrepreneurship can serve as a model for how a government can effectively spur entrepreneurship in a country through the establishment of a "Center of Excellence." Although the Queen Rania Center exists independent of another institution, it is also possible to develop such a Center in conjunction with a university (such as the Center for Entrepreneurial Excellence at the Institute for Business Administration in Karachi, Pakistan). USAID can play a key role in providing financial support and technical assistance to such institutions; in fact, both IBA Karachi and the Queen Rania Center have already benefited from USAID support.

Key Questions for Program Design

Budget

- Does your budget allow implementation of a multi-faceted entrepreneurship program?

Entrepreneurship Components

- Which of the six components will be inclusive of the proposed entrepreneurship program?
  - Identify
  - Train
  - Connect and Sustain
  - Fund
  - Enable
  - Celebrate

Lessons Learned for Future USG Assistance

1. Programs to support entrepreneurship, and in particular incubators, should be comprehensive and pair funding and linkages to support networks with training activities.

2. Make sure there is a suitable and appropriate management structure in place prior to making any type of financial investment.

3. Donor-created incubators often do not work efficiently nor do they prove to have sustainable impact.

Entrepreneurship Development Firms Contact List

Organization	Contact Name	Email	Website	Focus Area(s)
Citi Foundation	Irena Shiba, Program Officer	Shibai@citi.com	www.citigroup.com/citi/ foundation/	Mixed Model *(Primary)*

Organization Summary

Citi Foundation, the corporate foundation of Citi Group, fund projects in 86 countries where Citi Group operates and last awarded $68 million in grants for development projects. They work with local partners to implement these projects, which focus primarily on financial inclusion and training, microfinance, climate change and sustainability, and business education. An example of one of their long-standing initiatives is Junior Achievement Europe, in Turkey. This grant supports the expansion of the Company program into three new cities across the country targeting 2,200 students in 110 schools. The program trains students between the ages of 15-18 through the entire business cycle. Students determine a product or service they wish to sell, set up a company, raise capital, market and sell their product and, at the end, liquidate operations. Students work in groups to develop a small business and are supported by a business mentor throughout the process. Student teams participate in regional trade fairs and a national competition, with winning teams proceeding to compete at the European level.

Organization	Contact Name	Email	Website	Focus Area(s)
CMEA Capital	Faysal Sohail, General Partner	faysal@cmea.com	www.cmea.com	Mixed Model *(Primary)*

Organization Summary

CMEA Capital is a venture capital firm based in San Francisco that invests in entrepreneurs and companies focused in the energy (alternative energies), information technology (software, semiconductors and emerging internet technologies), and life sciences (drug development, medical device and diagnostics companies) sectors. Investments range from $0.5 million to $50 million and are made to individuals and companies across the business spectrum, from first-time novices to serial entrepreneurs. A key feature of inherent in its operations is the belief that successful entrepreneurs require more than just ideas and capital. Thus, in addition to finding sources of funding, CMEA Capital provides entrepreneurs the opportunity to form relationships with a network of corporate partners.

Organization	Contact Name	Email	Website	Focus Area(s)
Goldman Sachs *10,000 Women*	Noa Meyer, Program Director	noa.meyer@gs.com	www. goldmansachs.com/ citizenship/10000women	Mixed Model *(Primary)*

Organization Summary

10,000 Women is a five-year investment funded by Goldman Sachs (GS) to train business and finance management skills to underserved women around the world. GS partners with dozens of nonprofits, development organizations and universities to implement these trainings. To date, they have worked in 22 countries and trained nearly 5,000 women. Topics taught include, but are not limited to, asset management, strategic planning, accounting, accessing capital, marketing, and business plan writing. Its list of partners includes organizations such as CARE, Ashoka, Harvard, Georgetown, London Business School, American University in Cairo, and many others.

Organization	Contact Name	Email	Website	Focus Area(s)
Oasis 500	Salwa Katkhuda, Investment Manager	salwa@oasis500.com	www.oasis500.com	Mixed Model *(Primary)*

Organization Summary

Oasis 500 is a for-profit investment company that offers multiple services to entrepreneurs, including boot camp training, equity financing, and links to investors. They focus on the ICT, digital media, and mobile segments. Oasis 500's model begins with an open invitation to entrepreneurs through radio stations and events. Interested entrepreneurs submit their idea in a brief explanation, and the top individuals are offered boot camp training in topics as how to start a business, finance, marketing of technology products, and pitching to investors. The boot camp, set up as an NGO, is funded through company sponsorships, such as Orange (telecom) and Arab Bank. Training is provided by internal Oasis 500 staff, and top entrepreneurs are connected with an investor network.

Organization	Contact Name	Email	Website	Focus Area(s)
Queen Rania Center for Entrepreneurship	Farhan Kaladeh, Executive Director	http://www.qrce. org/?q=contact	www.qrce.org	Mixed Model *(Primary)*

Organization Summary

The Queen Rania Center is focused on improving the mindset toward entrepreneurship in Jordan. Their focus is primarily on technology fields, including ICT, clean technology (food, water, and energy), biotech/life sciences, as well as security and defense. Their focus is on the 3-4% of entrepreneurs that constitute true "growth entrepreneurs," whom they target through activities such as seminars, workshops, and business plan competitions. The Center's programs are targeted at entrepreneurs at different stages of development, and are matched with volunteer mentors and/or funders who may be able to support them.

Back to Top - Mixed Models   *Back to Resource List – Mixed Models*

Works Cited

Amorós, José Ernesto, Niels Bosma and Donna J. Kelley. Global Entrepreneurship Monitor 2010 Global Report. GEM, 2011.

Fogel, Daniel S., and Devi R. Gnyawali. "Environments for Entrepreneurship Development: Key Dimensions and Research Implications," Entrepreneurship: Theory and Practice. 18 (Summer): 43-62.

Gorman, Gary, Dennis Hanlon, and Wayne King. "Some Research Perspectives on Entrepreneurial Education, Enterprise Education and Education for Small business Management: A Ten-year Literature Review." International Small Business Journal. 13/3 (April-June): 56.

Hot Industries. Cognetics Inc. Cambridge, Massachusetts, 1995.

Naude, Wim. "Promoting Entrepreneurship in Developing Countries: Policy Changes." Policy Brief No. 4, UNU-WIDER. 2010.

Additional Publications/Reference Materials

Books and articles

Allen, Kathleen. Entrepreneurship For Dummies. For Dummies, 2000.
  • This work offers a step-by-step guide of various aspects associated with starting a business.

Berkery, Dermot. Raising Venture Capital for the Serious Entrepreneur. McGraw-Hill, 2007.
  • This book explains what it is that venture capitalists look for in a business plan, how they arrange financing for a company, and accordingly what an entrepreneur's basic strategies ought to be.

Bhide, Amar, Michael J. Roberts and Howard H. Stevenson. William A. Salhman, ed. The Entrepreneurial Venture. Harvard Business Press, 1999.
  • This text consists of a collection of readings by leading academics and practitioners in the field of entrepreneurship, covering a comprehensive range of relevant topics, from basic concepts to emerging issues.

Bornstein, David and Susan Davis. Social Entrepreneurship: What Everyone Needs to Know. Oxford University Press, 2010.
  • Developed in a Q & A format, this text offers a general overview of social entrepreneurship, with topics including what differentiates social entrepreneurs from their for-profit counterparts and some of the challenges organizations face.

Brinkerhoff, Peter C. Social Entrepreneurship: The Art of Mission-Based Venture Development. Wiley, 2000.
  • This work contends that non-profits ought to operate their organizations like businesses. Social Entrepreneurship addresses how to focus on community needs and wants, tap into funding sources, write a business plan, and appropriately balance the questions of mission and money.

Brodsky, Norm and Bo Burlingham. Street Smarts: An All-Purpose Tool Kit for New Entrepreneurs. Portfolio Trade, 2010.
  • Rather than focus on a set of formulas or rules, this book argues that there is a mentality necessary to be a successful entrepreneur. Street Smarts discusses this mentality, and the role it plays in solving problems and pursuing opportunities.

Collins, James, and William C. Lazier. <u>Beyond Entrepreneurship: Turning Your Business into an Enduring Great Company.</u> Prentice Hall, 1995.
  • This text consists of five key elements involved in guiding a company to success, as well as discussion of how to manage a company.

Drucker, Peter F. Innovation and Entrepreneurship. Harper Paperbacks, 2006.
  • This book analyzes the challenges and opportunities of America's entrepreneurial economy.

Farrell, Larry C. <u>Getting Entrepreneurial!: Creating and Growing Your Own Business in the 21st Century – Lessons From the World's Greatest Entrepreneurs.</u> Wiley, 2003.
  • Getting Entrepreneurial provides four central fundamentals that have guided many of the world's most successful entrepreneurs, and it discusses methods for product identification and vision development.

Gerber, Michael E. <u>The E-Myth Revisited: Why Most Small Businesses Don't Work and What to Do About It.</u> HarperCollins, 1995.
  • This book dispels common myths regarding starting businesses, and walks the reader through the various stages of developing a business.

Gold, Steven K. <u>Entrepreneur's Notebook: Practical Advice for Starting a New Business Venture.</u> Learning Ventures Press, 2006.
  • This work offers a tour of the start-up process, with a wide range of topics, including team building, writing a business plan, and financing.

Hawken, Paul. <u>Growing a Business.</u> Simon & Schuster, 1988.
  • This book discusses the importance of making a business unique, and something that only the entrepreneur is capable of producing. He further argues that the creation of something of value, not risk-taking, ought to be the purpose of entrepreneurship.

Hupalo, Peter. <u>Thinking Like An Entrepreneur: How To Make Intelligent Business Decisions That Will Lead To Success In Building And Growing Your Own Company.</u> HCM Publishing, 1999.
  • This book discusses how to adjust from an employee to company founder, and offers a set of tools needed to take control of one's financial destiny and think like an entrepreneur.

Kawasaki, Guy. <u>Enchantment: The Art of Changing Hearts, Minds, and Actions.</u> Portfolio Hardcover, 2011.
  • *Enchantment* is comprised of discussion on how to persuade others, through treatment of techniques and the use of successful case studies.

Kawasaki, Guy. <u>The Art of the Start: The Time-Tested, Battle-Hardened Guide for Anyone Starting Anything.</u> Portfolio Hardcover, 2004.
  • This text offers advice on how to launch products, services and companies, with discussion including branding, networking, recruiting, building buzz, and other topics.

Kennedy, Joe. <u>The Small Business Owner's Manual: Everything you Need to Know to Start Up and Run Your Business.</u> Career Press, 2005.
  • This text provides practical advice for new and established entrepreneurs, with information on how to obtain financing, sell products and services, advertise and obtain administrative efficiency.

Key, Stephen. <u>One Simple Idea: Turn Your Dreams into a Licensing Goldmine While Letting Others Do the Work</u>. McGraw-Hill, 2011.
  • *One Simple Idea* contains information on how inventors can turn their ideas into successful enterprises.

MacMillan, Ian and Rita Gunther McGrath. The Entrepreneurial Mindset: Strategies for Continuously Creating Opportunity in an Age of Uncertainty. Harvard Business Press, 2000.
- This work argues that an entrepreneur cannot employ conventional business thinking and be successful. It then offers a blueprint for thinking and acting in the entrepreneurial realm, to energize organizations and find tomorrow's opportunities.

Mullins, John. The New Business Road Test: What Entrepreneurs and Executives Should do Before Writing a Business Plan. FT Press, 2004.
- Intended as a tool for those considering starting a new business, *The New Business Road Test* makes it possible to gauge whether or not a business idea is feasible and provides advice on how to avoid commonly-made mistakes.

Murphy, Bill. The Intelligent Entrepreneur: How Three Harvard Business School Graduates Learned the 10 Rules of Successful Entrepreneurship. Henry Holt and Co., 2010.
- This work offers a narrative on how three HBS graduates successfully launched businesses upon their graduation.

Port; Michael and Carol Roth. The Entrepreneur Equation: Evaluating the Realities, Risks, and Rewards of Having Your Own Business. BenBella Books, 2011.
- This book discusses the questions that people ought to ask themselves when deciding whether or not to start a business, and offers advice concerning the key elements to success.

Price, Robert W. Roadmap to Entrepreneurial Success: Powerful Strategies for Building a High-Profile Business. AMACOM, 2004.
- This book focuses on how to succeed in the context of an uncertain environment. It focuses on a "path to profitability", with discussion on the necessary tools for entrepreneurs, and how to identify a business' value drivers.

Sahlman, William Andrews. Harvard Business Review on Entrepreneurship. Harvard Business Review Paperback Series, Feb 10, 1999.
- This review consists of a collection of articles related to entrepreneurship, with topics including strategies, financing, milestones and marketing, among others.

Shane, Scott Andrew. The Illusions of Entrepreneurship: The Costly Myths That Entrepreneurs, Investors, and Policy Makers Live By. Yale University Press, 2008.
- This book relies on data to determine who becomes an entrepreneur and why, how businesses are started, and what factors lead to success or failure.

Small Business Sourcebook, Edition 28. Gale Group, 2011. http://www.gale.cengage.com/servlet/BrowseSeriesServlet?region=9&imprint=000&titleCode=SMBS&edition
- This text, published annually, provides guidance on how to start a business, and provides profiles of both classic and small businesses.

Start Your Own Business: The Only Start-Up Book You'll Ever Need. Entrepreneur Press, 2010.
- This text offers startup essentials, as well as a view of what is necessary to survive the initial stages of starting a business. Topics include finding a target market, receiving financing, marketing products, and effectively using resources.

Urquhart-Brown, Susan. The Accidental Entrepreneur: The 50 Things I Wish Someone Had Told Me About Starting a Business. AMACOM, 2008.
- This book offers advice on what does and doesn't work when starting a business, with topics including information to know before starting, advice for developing business plans, marketing tips, and pitfalls to avoid.

Web resources

AllBusiness, http://www.allbusiness.com/
- *AllBusiness* is an online resource for small business, with tools and information concerning how to start, manage and grow businesses. Content includes daily news, blogs, and original feature stories, as well as special reports and videos.

Association of Small Business Development Centers, http://207.204.22.87/index.html
- This website consists of various content relevant to small businesses, including access to webinars, resources for small business owners, and content specific to various topics relevant to small businesses.

Business Owners Toolkit, http://www.toolkit.com/small_business_guide/index.aspx.
- This site offers a collection of documents concerning various processes associated with running a business, including starting and planning businesses, financial planning, and marketing.

Edward Lowe Foundation, http://edwardlowe.org/index.elf
- This website consists of information and educational opportunities for entrepreneurs who have passed the start-up phase, but have not reached full business maturity as a company.

Entrepreneur, http://www.entrepreneur.com/
- *Entrepreneur* offers a collection of information for entrepreneurs, with daily articles, as well as how-to guides, and growth strategies.

Foundation for Enterprise Development, http://www.fed.org/
- This is a site for innovative science and technology entrepreneurs containing small business resource lists, news and other information for entrepreneurs.

Global Entrepreneurship Monitor, http://www.gemconsortium.org/default.aspx
- *GEM* is an academic consortium that researches information relevant to entrepreneurs, with website content including datasets, research and national and global publications.

Harvard Business School: Entrepreneurship, http://www.hbs.edu/entrepreneurship/resources/
- HBS's entrepreneurship website includes resources, as well as guides about various aspects of entrepreneurship, including finding funders, writing a business plan, and recruiting staff.

Inc. Magazine, http://www.inc.com/
- This is the online format of *Inc. Magazine* (some articles are free, others require a subscription) with various articles pertaining to start-ups, business management, finance, and other entrepreneurial-related topics.

Kauffman Foundation, http://www.entrepreneurship.org/
- This site contains information about programs and resources relevant to entrepreneurship.

Stanford University's Entrepreneurship Corner, http://ecorner.stanford.edu/
- Stanford's *Entrepreneurship Corner* has 2000 free videos and podcasts concerning innovation and entrepreneurship from thought leaders in the field.

Startup Nation, http://www.startupnation.com/
- *Startup Nation* is a site to help entrepreneurs, with discussion of how to start a business, and a searchable database of tips and practical advice.

UC Berkeley Lester Center for Entrepreneurship, http://entrepreneurship.berkeley.edu/main/index.html
- While much of the information on this site is student-specific, it does include relevant content, including recordings of lectures about entrepreneurship best practices.

US Small Business Administration, http://archive.sba.gov/advo/research/
- This is the official site of the US Government Office committed to small businesses. Website content includes research on small businesses, data, and guides to topics relevant to small business owners.

Wicked Start, http://www.wickedstart.com/public_home
- This is a site to support startups, with personalized checklists, guidance from experts, and resources to plan and develop a new business.

USAID Project Summaries

Country	Date	Project	Implementing & Local Partners	Description of Activities	Links
Afghanistan	2006-2011	Capacity Development Program (CDP)	BearingPoint, Development Alternatives Inc. (DAI)	CDP builds upon existing programs and fills critical gaps to increase performance capacity of Afghan organizations in the government public, higher education and for-profit private sectors and nongovernmental organizations (NGOs). The project also enhances coordination and promotes uniform approaches across service providers; builds the capacity of organizations to attract and maintain competent staff; and develops a critical mass of skilled professionals necessary to allow public sector organizations to achieve objectives.	http://www.usaidcdp.org/about.htm
Afghanistan	2006-2009	Agriculture Rural Investment & Enterprise Strengthening (ARIES)	Academy for Educational Development (AED)	ARIES expanded access to financial services in the rural regions of Afghanistan, working to build a strong private sector foundation for a sustainable finance system. The project collaborated with local banks and cooperatives, provided assistance to the Microfinance Investment Support Facility of Afghanistan (MISFA), developed guarantee mechanisms to increase wholesale lending to microfinance institutions and small and medium enterprises, and supported an investment vehicle to provide growing enterprises with access to larger-scale debt investment. During the implementation period, ARIES established a total outstanding loan portfolio of $22 million and 75,000 active borrowers across 20 of Afghanistan's 34 provinces.	http://www.aed.org/Projects/ARIES.cfm http://pdf.usaid.gov/pdf_docs/PDACQ819.pdf
Afghanistan	2006-2009	Alternative Development Program/Eastern Region (ADP/E)	Development Alternatives Inc. (DAI)	ADP/E promoted sustainable regional economic development in the Eastern Region though a multi-pillar strategy with two primary objectives: 1) accelerate licit economic growth and business activity; and 2) help provide an immediate alternative source of income to poor households whose livelihoods depend, directly or indirectly, on the opium economy.	http://www.dai.com/work/project_detail.php?pid=98

Country	Date	Project	Implementing & Local Partners	Description of Activities	Links
Afghanistan	2005-2009	**Alternative Development Project for the Southern Region (ADP/S)**	Chemonics International Inc.	ADP/S focused on combating opium production by building capacity for licit agricultural trade, working with officials in the public and private sectors to establish linkages between Afghan pomegranate farmers and regional markets, and training agribusiness investors on profitability analysis and marketing techniques. Over the period of performance, the project installed and upgraded power grid and transportation infrastructure, constructed the largest agro-industrial park in the region, and mobilized the workforce through cash-for-work programs to accommodate increased agricultural production.	http://www.chemonics.com/ projects/submit_search_ contracts.aspx?showBack= 1&ckCurrent=1&selPractice= {E552FD52-30C8-4628-B9DB-61794AF461AD}
Afghanistan	2006-2012	**Small and Medium-Sized Enterprise Development (ASMED)**	Development Alternatives Inc. (DAI) *Nangarhar University, Jalalabad; Kabul University, Kabul*	ASMED provides business development services to small and medium-sized enterprises (SMEs) and their supporting private sector institutions. It advocates for policy reforms to eliminate barriers to establishing and sustaining successful businesses, supports the development of local business infrastructure, facilitates public-private partnerships, supports practical business training for private sector leaders, and facilitates internal and external market linkages for Afghan SMEs. Outcomes in entrepreneurship have included: creation of a strong advocacy capacity among business associations; provision of assistance to SMEs in identifying foreign companies wanting to invest in the Afghanistan economy and establishment of alliances with these firms; and internship programs implemented in collaboration with two universities to increase the private sector skill capacity of young professionals. Upon completion of a two-month business training course in requisite skills, 120 interns were matched with well-established, successful organizations and business people throughout the country.	http://www.dai.com/work/ project_detail.php?pid=134 http://afghanistan.usaid.gov/ en/USAID/Activity/32/ Afghanistan_Small_and_ Medium_Enterprise_ Development_ASMED

Country	Date	Project	Implementing & Local Partners	Description of Activities	Links
Afghanistan	2003-2006	**Rebuilding Agricultural Markets In Afghanistan Program (RAMP)**	Chemonics International Inc.	RAMP was a donor-funded initiative to support the agricultural sector and improve lives of Afghani rural inhabitants by increasing food supplies and food security, creating jobs, increasing incomes, and strengthening the competitiveness of agricultural production. The total value added to the agriculture sector over the course of the project was estimated at $1.7 billion. Results included: rehabilitation of agriculture infrastructure benefiting 490,000+ hectares of farmland; extension services for one million farmers; more than 580 km of improved farm to market road; poultry production and management for 28,000 village women; improved post-harvest facilities, vaccination/treatment of over 28 million livestock; disbursement of 28,000+ micro loans and establishment of linkages between farmers; processors and traders for domestic and international market specifications.	http://afghanistan.usaid.gov/en/Activity.9.aspx
Afghanistan	2002-2005	**Economic Governance in Afghanistan - Sustainable Economic Policy and Institutional Reform Support Program (SEPIRS)**	BearingPoint	SEPIRS aimed to implement and institutionalize trade policy and promotion, as well as institutional reforms in core macroeconomic and structural reform areas.	http://tcbdb.wto.org/trta_project.aspx?prjCode=201-0137-03-E&benHostId=116

88

Country	Date	Project	Implementing & Local Partners	Description of Activities	Links
Afghanistan/ Kosovo	2008-2010	**Community Development Agriculture Program in Paktia, Paktika, Khost, and Southeast Ghazni (CDA-P2K)**	ACDI/VOCA *Local Councils*	CDA-PK2 alleviated production constraints, linked products to markets that offered comparatively greater returns to local market sales, and promoted private sector investment in the agricultural system for the purpose of generating increased income and employment for communities in the P2K and southeastern Ghazni regions.	http://www.acdivoca.org/ acdivoca/PortalHub.nsf/ID/ afghanistanCDA
				Results included: implementation of a forage voucher program to distribute alfalfa seed to 12,000 farmers; creation of Farm Stores that reached 37,000+ rural producers; collaboration with a local finance institution to introduce a $485,000 loan product pilot program to reach rural smallholders; registration and provision of technical assistance to 25 associations with more than 12,300 members; and training for 12,701 farmers, producers and agricultural entrepreneurs.	
				The project also designed a framework for a small-scale strawberry business for 60 women, a grant program for 600 Kuchi women for breeding stock, a commercial livestock feeding business, a small-scale abattoir business, and the provision of initial training for 20 para-vets to serve 200,000 heads of livestock per year.	
Albania	2009-2014	**Technical Assistance for Competitive Enterprise Development**	Chemonics International Inc.	The program works with selected municipalities, industries, and enterprises to increase the ability of SMEs to compete in domestic and international markets by facilitating access to credit and technologies; strengthening trade and investment through technical assistance; and providing managerial and technical training on compliance with international standards for improved trade, as well as identifying and meeting market demands.	http://www.chemonics.com/ Projects/submit_search_ contracts.aspx?showBack =1&selPractice=%7BE55 2FD52-30C8-4628-B9DB-61794AF461AD%7D

Country	Date	Project	Implementing & Local Partners	Description of Activities	Links
Albania	2006-2008	**Junior Achievement Enterprise Education Program (JAEEP)**	Junior Achievement-Young Enterprise Europe (JA-YE Europe) *Ministry of Education*	JAEEP introduced enterprise and economic education to Albanian youth through partnerships between local businesses and schools. Topics included enterprise, entrepreneurship, and "economic literacy," focusing on the importance of market-driven economies; the role of business in the economy; the relevance of education in the workplace; the impact of economics on a child's future; and the commitment of business to social, environmental and ethical issues.	http://albania.usaid.gov/ shfaqart/48/57/Junior_Achievement_Enterprise_Education_Program.htm
Albania	2003-2008	**USAID Albania Competitiveness Program (EDEM)**	Development Alternatives Inc. (DAI)	EDEM sought to increase economic opportunity, raise the standard of living, and facilitate Albania's entrance into the global marketplace. The program worked to identify and rapidly develop industries and services that offered the most promise for growth and job creation, especially among SMEs, and assisted Albanian businesses by supporting efforts to implement management plans, marketing, and promoticnal strategies, develop new products, and upgrade technologies. During its initial three years, EDEM provided assistance to four industry sectors: meat processors, herbs and spices, tourism, and fruits and vegetables consolidators and processors. In addition, EDEM assisted the Albanian Center for International Trade in the footwear industry.	http://www.dai.com/ work/project_detail.php?pid=5&x=12&y=8
Albania	2003-2007	**Albanian Centre for International Trade (ACIT)**	*Institute of Contemporary Studies (ISB),* *Ministry of Economy, Trade and Energy*	ACIT pursued quality improvement of trade policies in Albania, and the utilization of opportunities created by trade liberalization and integration for the benefit of citizen and society.	http://albania.usaid.gov/?fq=b renda&m=shfaqart&aid=41& arkat=52&tit=Albanian_Cen-ter_for_International_Trade_(ACIT)&qi=qi2

Country	Date	Project	Implementing & Local Partners	Description of Activities	Links
Albania	2007	**Value Chain Case Studies**	Chemonics International Inc.	Two studies were conducted. The first was based on previous agricultural work in Afghanistan and focused on two value chains at opposite ends of the economic spectrum: poultry, which is a subsistence activity, and raisins and grapes, which are high-value crops produced mainly for export. The second study was based on previous business development work in Kosovo and focused on the dairy industry. In both cases, value-chain development and analyses were used to rebuild markets in a post-conflict environment. The studies were created to be useful tools in efforts to fuel economic growth in post-conflict countries.	http://www.chemonics.com/projects/submit_search_contracts.aspx?showBack=1&ckCurrent=0&selRegion={626D2F6F-1E53-41B6-9090-C5E2BC1C4E33}
Albania	1996	**Students in Free Enterprise (SIFE)**		USAID gave support to the Albanian chapter of SIFE, providing students and faculty with knowledge on how a market economy operates, skills needed to participate in a competitive global economy, how to succeed as an entrepreneur, personal financial management, and ethical business practices. Participants had the opportunity to form linkages with firms and learn practical aspects of business.	http://www.sifealbania.org/index.php?faqe=sifeut1
Armenia	2000-2007	**Agribusiness Small and Medium-Sized Enterprise Market Development Program (ASME) Business Assistance and Development**	Development Alternatives Inc. (DAI)	ASME increased market opportunities for small and medium-sized agribusinesses by: 1) providing technical support to the Government of Armenia to strengthen its surveillance, laboratory diagnosis, and monitoring capabilities; 2) assisting private poultry producers to improve flock monitoring and biosafety practices and prepare to respond effectively to outbreaks; and 3) coordinating all communications activities among donor organizations and government ministries and developing communication materials. Initial efforts were exclusively targeted at agribusiness enterprises, but were later broadened to include non-farm rural enterprises, resulting in a strengthened rural business service provider network and commercial links between the providers and their private clients. The project team expanded its client base and had notable success in encouraging local industry association development.	http://www.dai.com/work/project_detail.php?pid=6

Country	Date	Project	Description of Activities	Implementing & Local Partners	Links
Azerbaijan	2004-2007		This project was designed to stimulate rural economic growth by helping farmers and small medium enterprises increase their sales and create new employment opportunities by generating and strengthen market-linkages, improving technical and business skills, and facilitating access to grants and leasing institutions. The program focused on high impact interventions, working through processors, traders and wholesalers to create backward linkages with 15,615 small holder producers. Assistance was given to a total of 57 clients and 63 leasing clients during the implementation period.	Chemonics International Inc.	http://pdf.usaid.gov/pdf_docs/PDACM842.pdf
Azerbaijan	2003-2008	**Rural Enterprise Competitiveness Program**	The Rural Enterprise Competitive Program raised rural incomes and agriculture productivity by increasing the volume and quality of fresh and processed agricultural products, and as well as the volume of value added products in domestic and export markets. The project also provided income benefits for a broad range of producers and processors and enabled Azeri agricultural products to displace imports and reach export markets by introducing the competitiveness paradigm in the agricultural and agri-business clusters of Azerbaijan's economy.	Pragma Corp.	http://www.pragmacorp.com/recp.htm http://www.usaid.gov/locations/europe_eurasia/press/success/2008-05-05.html
Azerbaijan	2008	**"Oil Revenues and State Expenditures"**	USAID supported a roundtable on "Oil Revenues and State Expenditures" to examine transparency and efficiency in the management of oil revenues in Azerbaijan, bringing together approximately 40 representatives of Parliament, various ministries, the State Oil Fund, international and local NGOs, economic experts and journalists.	Eurasia Foundation, Entrepreneurship Development Foundation	http://www.usaid.gov/locations/europe_eurasia/press/success/2007-05-25.html
Azerbaijan	2007-2010	**Enterprise Development and Training Program**	The Enterprise Development and Training Program supported small and medium-sized Azeri companies in the development of local supplier processes that met relevant international quality, health, safety, security and environmental (HSSE) standards, ISO certifications, and BP's specific requirements.	ACDIVOCA	http://www.acdivoca.org/acdivoca/PortalHub.nsf/ID/azerbaijanEDTP

Country	Date	Project	Implementing & Local Partners	Description of Activities	Links
Bangladesh	1997-2005	**The Job Opportunities and Business Support (JOBS)**	IRIS Center, UMD	The USAID-funded JOBS program created sustainable employment by helping small, micro, and medium entrepreneurs grow their enterprises. Building on eight years of success of the project, JOBS Trust Bangladesh was founded in 2005 as a local multi-donor funded entity. It continues to operate as an integrated private sector development program, providing support to Bangladeshi enterprises with the aim of increasing employment opportunities, especially for some of the most marginalized populations in Bangladesh. JOBS ICT Private Ltd. was established in 2006, JOBS International Inc., USA in 2007, and JOBS International Private Ltd. Pakistan in 2008.	http://www.usaid.gov/our_work/cross-cutting_programs/wid/snapshot/ane/bangladesh/bang_jobs.html http://jobs-group.org/
Belarus, Moldova, Ukraine	2000-2006	**Support to Micro, Small and Medium Enterprise Development (BIZPRO)**	Development Alternatives Inc. (DAI)	BIZPRO was designed to help Ukrainian enterprises compete in foreign and domestic markets by working at the enterprise, sector, and policy/legal level through entrepreneur hotlines, seminars, and business networks. In Moldova, the program contributed to economic development by providing assistance that improved the ability of small and medium-sized enterprises (SMEs) to operate and compete in local and external markets. In Belarus, the project implemented Certified Accounting Professional (CAP)/Certified International Professional Accountant (CIPA) programs and engaged a local think tank to provide economic analysis designed to generate and inform public-private dialogue.	http://www.dai.com/work/project_detail.php?pid=167&x=5&y=14 http://pdf.usaid.gov/pdf_docs/PDACL497.pdf

93

Country	Date	Project	Implementing & Local Partners	Description of Activities	Links
Bosnia	2005-2009	Poverty Reduction by Increasing the Competitiveness of Enterprise	Chemonics International Inc.	The program worked to move Bosnia's private sector from underperforming to globally competitive through provision of technical assistance and managerial advice to entrepreneurs and associations. Working with the private and public sectors, the project team selected three sectors on which to focus and developed models for other sectors. Within those areas, the project team trained businesses and entrepreneurs in management, marketing, finance and accounting, and operations. The team also introduced new processing technologies and management systems and encouraged linkages between the private sector and research institutions, including universities.	http://www.chemonics.com/Projects/submit_search_contracts.aspx?showBack=1&selPractice=%7BE55 2FD52-30C8-4628-B9DB-61794AF461AD%7D
Bosnia	2005-2009	Cluster Competitiveness Activity (CCA)	Emerging Markets Group Ltd.	CCA pursued an increase in the rate of economic growth in BiH by working with interested stakeholders in the wood processing/forestry and tourism sectors to raise productivity, profits and employment.	http://www.emergingmarketsgroup.com/Services.aspx?ServiceID=6179b73f-fd12-446d-9de8-50a38826319 6&Article=EMG+Helps+to+Improve+Competitiveness+in+Bosnia+and+Herzegovina
Bosnia and Herzegovina	2005	"BiH Youth, Let's Make Our Future!" youth conference	The Youth Information Agency (OIA)	The event engaged 530 youth and gave participants a sense of the practical skills needed to find a job, get an internship, or open a business.	http://www.usaid.gov/locations/europe_eurasia/press/success/a_decade_after_dayton.html
Bulgaria	2005+	Center for Entrepreneurship and Executive Development (CEED) Bulgaria	Small Enterprise Assistance Fund (SEAF)	CEED Bulgaria is part of the international network of CEED centers with offices in Bulgaria, Macedonia, Romania, Montenegro and Slovenia. The objective of CEED is to expand to other South East European countries, to energize and empower entrepreneurs, and help them grow their businesses.	http://www.en.ceed-bulgaria.org/web/default.aspx

Country	Date	Project	Implementing & Local Partners	Description of Activities	Links
Cambodia	2002-2005	**Center of Entrepreneurship and Development**	Fisk University, United Negro College Fund Special Programs	This program developed a Center for Entrepreneurship and Development at the National Institute of Management in Phnom Penh.	http://egateg.usaidallnet.gov/term/tags/sme
Cambodia	2005-2008	**Strengthening Micro, Small and Medium Enterprises in Cambodia (Cambodia MSMEs)**	Development Alternatives Inc. (DAI)	The objective of Cambodia MSMEs was to upgrade micro, small, and medium enterprises in Cambodia, as well as the value chains in which they operate, by building relationships between value chain actors, improving producers' technical skills, helping MSMEs access markets and credit, and improving the provincial business environment.	
Central Asia: Kazakhstan, Kyrgyz Repub-lic, Tajikistan, Uzbekistan, Turkmenistan	2002-2006	**Enterprise Development Project in Central Asia**	Pragma Corp.	The project provided entrepreneurs with the opportunity to acquire business information, knowledge, and skills through the implementation of its seven inter-related major components: 1) Business Training, 2) Accounting Reform, 3) Business Advisory Services, 4) Regional Trade Promotion, 5) Association Development, 6) Quality Management Center (Kazakhstan only), and 7) Cross-Cutting Related Activities. The ultimate objective of the project was to enhance the productivity and competitiveness of local companies to enable them to compete in domestic, regional, and international markets. Technical assistance provided by the EDP was delivered through 12 Enterprise Development Centers (EDCs) located throughout the region.	http://www.pragmacorp.com/edp.htm
East Africa	2009-2013	**Competitiveness and Trade Expansion Project**	Chemonics International Inc.	The Competitiveness and Trade Expansion Project builds on the success of the Regional Agricultural Trade Expansion Support program (RATES) program, stimulating economic development through increased trade and competitiveness in regional and global markets. Operating from a regional platform, the project is working to improve the enabling environment for trade in East and Central Africa by: harmonizing regional trade and transit policies and procedures; developing financial markets; providing support to private sector associations to strengthen value chains; and building the capacity of regional businesses to take advantage of preferential trading opportunities under the African Growth and Opportunity Act.	http://www.chemonics.com/Projects/submit_search_contracts.aspx?showBack=1&selPractice=%7BE552FD52-30C8-4628-B9DB-61794AF461AD%7D

Country	Date	Project	Implementing & Local Partners	Description of Activities	Links
Egypt	1996-2009	**Commodity Import Program (CIP)**		The Commodity Import Program (CIP) was intended to foster a competitive private sector in Egypt, in addition to assisting U.S. exporters. The program also supports the government of Egypt and USAID activities and expenses in Egypt. Since 1992, Congress has appropriated at least $200 million per year for the CIP. In 1998, the United States negotiated a reduction in its economic assistance to Egypt, including the CIP, through fiscal year 2009.	http://www.usaideconomic.org. eg/CIP/Home.asp
Egypt	2005-2008	**Capacity Building Programme**	Development Alternatives Inc. (DAI)	The program contributed to private sector development in Egypt and stimulated and strengthened the capacity of the Egyptian financial sector by providing services to private small and medium-sized enterprises.	http://www.dai.com/work/ project_detail.php?pid=142
Egypt	2005-2007	**ICT Entrepreneurship Program**	Nathan Associates Inc.	The ICT Entrepreneurship Program in Egypt endeavored to increase the nation's competitiveness in ICT global markets. The project facilitated partnerships between Egyptian institutions and U.S. institutions, and provided training in advanced finance, entrepreneurial management, and ICT management so Egypt's entrepreneurs had the opportunity to grasp and apply the fundamentals of business financing. The project founded a "training of trainers program" and developed business plans for U.S.-based market development centers. It also trained financial analysts and established a free-standing private corporation—the ICT Business Development Center—in Cairo.	http://d178251.u69.bachcsi. com/projects-and-cases/egypt-ict-entrepreneurship-program-2005%E2%80%932007
Egypt	2006	**Egypt ICT and Tourism "While in Egypt Stay Connected"**	Emerging Markets Group Ltd. *Ministry of Communications and Information Technology*	The "While in Egypt Stay Connected" project was designed to expand connectivity and promote global competitiveness in the Egyptian tourism sector, as well as enhance Egypt's image as a regional ICT hub, strengthen the environment for trade and investment, evaluate technology and service-provider business model alternatives, and implement pilot initiatives.	http://psp.emergingmarkets-group.com/home_etourism. aspx?siteId=ab1fbe66-c00f-4b93-b538-27322b76c346

Country	Date	Project	Implementing & Local Partners	Description of Activities	Links
Egypt, India, Indonesia, Morocco, Pakistan, Philippines	2005-2010	**The Education and Employment (EEA) Alliance**	International Youth Foundation	EEA improved and expanded education and employment opportunities for disadvantaged and unemployed youth in six countries in the Middle East and Asia. Supported by USAID and a wide array of corporate, foundation, and other donors, EEA forged partnerships on multiple levels (global, national, and local), leveraging the expertise and resources of diverse partners to lay the groundwork for sustaining and scaling up interventions. In India, EEA supported innovative educational technology initiatives to improve the learning outcomes of students. In other countries, it offered comprehensive learning packages, combining technical/ vocational and life skills, entrepreneurship development, on-the-job training, and job placement or enterprise development support. Programs focused on addressing the unique needs of out-of-school and at-risk youth. Over the course of the project, partnerships were forged with over 320 multi-sectoral organizations in support of 43 pilot projects, benefitting more than one million children and youth; the Alliance's approach demonstrated improved program quality, relevance to private sector needs, and strong scalability and sustainability prospects; more than 29,000 youth participated in employability skills training interventions, with a 87% completion rate. 56% of program graduates secured jobs or set up small businesses, and 80% percent of the new entrepreneurs surveyed reported profits.	http://www.iyfnet.org/EEA
El Salvador	2008-2012	**Productive Development Program, Millennium Challenge Account**	Chemonics International Inc.	The Productive Development Program works to increase productivity, profitability, and competitiveness of value chains in the agriculture, dairy, forestry, tourism, and other sectors in El Salvador's rural northern zone. The project supports the development of profitable and sustainable business ventures, with a primary focus on assisting low-income farmers and micro, small, and medium-sized agricultural enterprises to shift to high-value activities. The project also provides business development support for MSMEs in tourism, handicrafts, and other relevant non-agricultural. The project expects to increase average real net incomes by 15	http://www.chemonics.com/Projects/submit_search_contracts.aspx?showBack=1&selPractice=%7BE55 2FD52-30C8-4628-B9DB-61794AF461AD%7D

Country	Date	Project	Implementing & Local Partners	Description of Activities	Links
				percent for more than 9,500 beneficiaries in the northern zone and create at least 7,800 full-time-equivalent new jobs.	
Georgia	2002-2009	**AgVANTAGE Project (Formerly SAVE: Support Added-Value Enterprises)**	Social Impact Inc. International Executive Service Corps (IESC)	AgVANTAGE worked to increase Georgia's economic growth rate and lower the country's trade deficit through expanded production, sale and exports of added-value agricultural products. During the implementation period, the project was reformulated to directly assist private-sector enterprises and associations, improve the financial environment of the agriculture/agribusiness system, and provide policy assistance and support to the Ministry of Agriculture. Over 120 firms within 20 market chains received project assistance. 63 enterprises received grants and technical assistance, generating a cumulative sales total of $37.7M, creating 1887 new jobs, and purchasing raw products from 37,000 farmers. Key markets to emerge from AgVANTAGE efforts were Ukraine, Germany, Poland, Kazakhstan, Baltic States and the U.S.	http://pdf.usaid.gov/pdf_docs/PDACR900.pdf
Georgia	2005-2009	**SME Support Project**		Through its grants mechanism, the SME Support Project developed a comprehensive TA program for universities and other educational institutions to provide a state-of-the-art entrepreneurship training program, with particular focus on youth, women and minorities.	http://egateg.usaidallnet.gov/sme-support-project
Georgia	2011-2015	**New Economic Opportunities (NEO)**	Chemonics International Inc.	The New Economic Opportunities Initiative (NEO) assists 84 Georgian rural communities by enhancing local economic development planning processes, capacity building to improve entrepreneurial skills and strengthen market linkages, and engage in small-scale infrastructure projects. The project provides assistance to local governments, enterprises, and individuals to increase rural incomes and reduce poverty levels and food security. NEO also works with internally displaced persons (IDP) communities to enable them to sustainably maintain their households.	http://www.chemonics.com/Projects/submit_search_contracts.aspx?showBack=1&selPractice=%7BE552FD52-30C8-4628-B9DB-61794AF461AD%7D

Country	Date	Project	Implementing & Local Partners	Description of Activities	Links
Global	2006-2011	**Business Growth Initiative (BGI)**	Weidemann Associates, Inc.	BGI seeks to provide technical leadership in enterprise development for USAID, for its development partners, and for the wider communities of practice in enterprise development. It is meant to provide both direct and indirect assistance through project designs, project evaluations, research, technical briefs, workshops and seminars and through pilot demonstration projects. One of the primary aims of the BGI project is to assist USAID professionals and staff engaged in enterprise development activities to perform tasks more effectively, while promoting best practices in project implementation.	http://www.weidemannassoc. com/BusinessGrowthInitiative. aspx
Global	2002-2007	**Accelerated Microenterprise Advancement Project: Business Development Services (AMAP BDS)**	ACDI/VOCA	The goal of AMAP BDS was to increase incomes in poor communities and promote economic growth by enhancing performance and thereby the competitiveness of micro and small enterprises. AMAP BDS sustainably linked enterprises to productive markets. To address growth constraints all along the value chain, AMAP BDS covered a range of solutions and services, including market access, product development, technology support services, and interventions to strengthen the legal, regulatory and policy environment. AMAP BDS Task Orders Included: · India Growth-Oriented Microenterprise Development Program (GMED) · Accelerated Microenterprise Advancement Project-Business Development Services Knowledge and Practice II (AMAP BDS K&P II) · Value Chain Development for Conflict-Affected Environments Kenya · Accelerated Microenterprise Advancement Project-Business Development Services Knowledge and Practice I (AMAP BDS K&P I) · Haiti Value Chain Analysis	http://www.acdivoca.org/ acdivoca/portalhub.nsf/ID/ globalAMAPBDS

Country	Date	Project	Implementing & Local Partners	Description of Activities	Links
Haiti	2006-2009	**Support to Haiti's Microfinance, Small and Medium Enterprises Sector (Haiti MSME)**	Development Alternatives Inc. (DAI)	Haiti MSME leveraged prior USAID project successes to reach a target population that included both potential generators of income and livelihoods (rural and agricultural micro, small, and medium-sized enterprises and market-oriented enterprises) and the poor and vulnerable populations (out-of-school youth, HIV/AIDS-affected populations, women, and rural populations).	http://egateg.usaidallnet.gov/ support-haitis-microfinance-small-and-medium-enterpris-es-sector-haiti-msme
India	2003-2009	**Quality Education and Skills Training (QUEST) Alliance**		QUEST is a public-private alliance initiated by USAID to demonstrate innovations in effective and responsible use of existing and emerging educational technologies (ET) and engage in research/advocacy in order to enhance the quality of education and vocational/life skills training for disadvantaged children and youth. In 2004, QUEST was absorbed by the six-nation Education and Employment Alliance (EEA) activity funded by the GDA. USAID's vision was for QUEST to evolve into an independent and sustainable entity, generating and managing its own funds without USAID and IYF support. By the end of September 2009, QUEST aimed to establish itself as an independent and credible resource organization in the field of ET.	http://www.usaid.gov/in/our_ work/health/education_doc3. htm
India	2007-2009	**Small and Medium-Sized Enterprise (SME) Development Program**	Development Alternatives Inc. (DAI)	The SME Development Program in India facilitated linkages between the SMEs and business development and finance services providers.	http://egateg.usaidallnet.gov/ small-and-medium-sized-enterprise-sme-development-program
India	2006-2009	**Information Communication Technology for Small Enterprise Capacity Building Program**	ACDI/VOCA, Infosys Technologies	This program developed ICT enabled applications to improve the efficiency of private sector extension services and fresh produce supply chain management in India. The award was based primarily on the achievements of ACDI/VOCA's Growth Oriented Micro-Enterprise Development (GMED) program, which focused on the integration of smallholder fresh fruit and vegetable (FFV) farmers into organized retail supply chains, as well as the significant improvement of the operations of these chains.	http://pdf.usaid.gov/pdf_docs/ PDACN993.pdf

Country	Date	Project	Implementing & Local Partners	Description of Activities	Links
				During the implementation period, 550 farmers from the Nandani Cooperative Society were integrated into organized commercial supply chains and produced for leading retailers. Farm-to-Market losses declined to less than 10% in many cases, and applications offered better control over stock and inventory costs.	
Indonesia	2006-2011	**Agribusiness Market and Support Activity (AMARTA)**	Development Alternatives, Inc. (DAI)	AMARTA assists the Government of Indonesia to promote a robust Indonesian agribusiness system that will contribute to Indonesian employment, growth, and prosperity. The project works with private businesses, farmers and other actors to improve efficiency, productivity, and product quality in nine value chains, and also assembles national actors to improve the agribusiness enabling environment. The AMARTA value chain interventions have been implemented throughout Indonesia using an ambitious outreach, awareness, and education program, incorporating government agencies, alliances of agribusiness enterprises, agribusiness associations and business service providers.	http://www.amarta.net/amarta/EN.aspx?mn=A1&lang=EN
Indonesia	2005-2009	**SENADA**	Development Alternatives, Inc. (DAI)	SENADA's objective is to generate economic growth in jobs and income, focusing on increasing competitiveness of light manufacturing industries: footwear, furniture, auto parts, garments, home accessories and information, and communications technology (ICT).	http://www.senada.or.id/new/ http://www.dai.com/work/project_detail.php?pid=113
Indonesia	2005	Economic Revitalization Program in Indonesia's Aceh Province	CHF International	The program promoted economic revitalization, self-sufficiency through post-Tsunami assistance.	http://www.chfinternational.org/node/21172

Country	Date	Project	Implementing & Local Partners	Description of Activities	Links
Indonesia	1992+	Emerging Markets Development Advisors Program	Institute of International Education (IIE) Volunteers for Economic Growth Alliance (VEGA)	The Emerging Markets Development Advisers Program (EMDAP), formerly known as the "Free Market Development Advisors Program (FMDAP)" was initiated in 1992. Since then, more than 170 Advisers have participated in the program, providing assistance to more than 120 businesses and organizations in 45 USAID-assisted countries. EMDAP advisers -- all students and recent graduates of U.S. MBA or Masters programs -- represent 70 U.S. graduate schools.	http://www.emdap.org/index.shtml
Indonesia	2005-2008	Reducing Barriers to Markets (PROMIS)	The Asia Foundation	PROMIS was a grant to support long-term technical assistance, short-term technical assistance, limited commodity support, and domestic and international training and conferences.	http://indonesia.usaid.gov/en/Activity.135.aspx
Iraq		Iraqi Youth Initiative	Louis Berger Group, Inc.	The Iraqi Youth Initiative focuses on the creation of opportunity for Iraqi youth aged 18-35. The Youth Initiative seeks to collaborate and extend the reach of existing institutions, facilitate the establishment of new businesses, promote the learning of trades, and encourage youth to explore new professions, so that they may earn salaries and profits to generate additional employment. The Initiative provides three main resources in entrepreneurship: Youth Entrepreneurship Resource Center (YERC), Youth Entrepreneurship Access to Finance (YEAF), and Youth Employment Promotion (YEP). More than 5,000 youths between the ages of 18 and 35 are projected to benefit from the program, which is expected to create 2,500 full-time jobs. Individual and group start-up loans are available to eligible individuals seeking to start their own businesses. Entrepreneurship training is selective and rigorous, and includes classroom workshops, one-on-one consultations, mentoring by experienced business planners and guidance from microfinance officials who can approve youth friendly loans.	http://www.iraqiyouthinitiative.org/en

Country	Date	Project	Implementing & Local Partners	Description of Activities	Links
Iraq	2006-2011	**Tatweer**	Management Systems International	USAID/ Tatweer (USAID's National Capacity Development program) increases the effectiveness of Iraqi ministries through reform of internal operational systems and inclusion of best practices and international standards. The Program develops public management skills, improves operating systems, and institutionalizes training activities at national and provincial levels. Core public administration areas include contract and procurement management, human resource management, project management, leadership and communication, strategic planning and information technology. The project aims to increase domestic sales and economic development by SMEs through improved quality, management systems, technology, and human resources.	http://www.tatweer-iraq.com
Jordan	2006-2011	**Sustainable Achievement of Business Expansion and Quality (SABEQ)**		SABEQ works to increase financial integrity, oversight and broadened capital markets; expand trade and investment; remove government constraints to achieve private sector competitiveness and enhance productivity.	http://www.sabeq-jordan.org/Sabeq_Public/main_Sabeq_Public_master.aspx?site_id=1&Page_id=2&REGION=1&LANG=3
Jordan	2002-2006	**Achievement of Market-Friendly Initiatives and Results Program (AMIR II)**	Chemonics International Inc.	Building on the success of its predecessor, AMIR II endeavored to develop a more favorable environment for business and investment by providing technical assistance and training. The focus was on micro enterprise, business management, information and communication technology, and private sector policy reforms (investment promotion, trade policy, customs reform, capital markets, etc.).	http://jordan.usaid.gov/project_disp.cfm?id=88
Jordan	1998-2002	**Access to Microfinance & Improved Implementation of Policy Reform (AMIR I)**	Chemonics International Inc.	AMIR I supported Jordan's entrepreneurs by helping to establish a sound, sustainable small-loan industry and by working to improve access to services that help people start and run their businesses.	http://www.usaid.gov/stories/jordan/fp_jordan_khawla.html http://pdf.usaid.gov/pdf_docs/PNADA413.pdf

Country	Date	Project	Implementing & Local Partners	Description of Activities	Links
Jordan	1999-2001	**Economic Opportunities for Jordanian Youth (INJAZ)**	Save the Children	INJAZ provides for the creation of partnerships between the private sector and educators throughout Jordan to help empower youth, introduce them to entrepreneurship, and provide them with new employment options beyond the traditional public sector. The program is based on the "Junior Achievement Worldwide" model and is targeted at Jordanian youth between the ages of 15 and 24. INJAZ offers employment skills needed in a modern economy through over 1,200 volunteers from 100 private sector organizations. INJAZ began as a USAID-funded project, and spun off in 2001 to become an independent non-profit organization under the Patronage of Her Majesty Queen Rania Al Abdullah II.	http://jordan.usaid.gov/ project_disp.cfm?id=81 http://www.injaz.org.jo/
Kazakhstan	2006-2010	**Kazakhstan Small Business Development (KSBD)**	Pragma Corporation	KSBD's objective was to increase the Government of Kazakhstan's knowledge of international best practices and lessons learned in implementing SME support programs, transfer capacity to the Government of Kazakhstan and indigenous institutions, manage and evaluate entrepreneurship development programs, and promote a sound development of a network of small business service providers to foster growth of SMEs.	http://www.pragmacorp.com/ ksbd.htm
Kazakhstan, Kyrgyzstan, Tajikistan and Turkmenistan	2004-2007	**Business and Economics Education Project (BEE)**	Carana Corporation	The Business and Economics Education Project in Central Asia (BEE) encouraged educational institutions to be more responsive to business needs, while promoting government education reforms in Kazakhstan, Kyrgyzstan, Tajikistan and Turkmenistan. CARANA tapped Central Asian firms and NGOs to support education reform through cost sharing and direct linkages with universities. During the life of the project, BEE piloted 12 university career, entrepreneurship and marketing research centers, as well as regional internship and scholarship programs. It set up a regional education association for advocacy and faculty training, university advisory boards and a major fund-raising campaign. Nearly 100 separate contributors paid for 29 percent of the total cost, demonstrating a strong vested interest in education reform. BEE built on the accomplishments of a previous USAID project, EdNet, which had	http://www.carana.com/ projects/regions/projects- by-region-europe-and- eurasia/198 http://www.usaid.gov/ locations/europe_eurasia/ press/success/2006-07-20. html

Country	Date	Project	Implementing & Local Partners	Description of Activities	Links
				established a Regional Education Network Association (REGENA) to support business and economics education programs.	
Kazakhstan, Kyrgyz Republic, Tajikistan, Turkmenistan, Uzbekistan	2007-2011	**Regional Agricultural Linkages (AgLinks)**	Development Alternatives, Inc. (DAI)	AgLinks boosts market-driven productivity at the farm level and improves market linkages to upgrade agribusiness value chains. The program develops the capacity of local service providers to provide farmer production assistance in response to market demand and to ameliorate choke points in the market linkages between producers and value chain buyers.	http://egateg.usaidallnet.gov/ regional-agricultural-linkages-aglinks
Kazakhstan, Kyrgyzstan, Tajikistan, and Uzbekistan	2001-2006	**SME Trade Facilitation Initiative**	Pragma Corporation	The SME Trade Facilitation Initiative functioned to improve the trade and investment environment for small and medium-sized enterprises. Activities focused on the reduction of investment constraints, trade facilitation, accession to and active participation in the World Trade Organization and the adoption of international practices in the areas of Metrology, Accreditation, Standardization, and Quality.	http://www.pragmacorp.com/ sme.htm
Kazakhstan, the Kyrgyz Republic, and Tajikistan	2006-2010	**Business Environment Improvement Project (BEI)**	Pragma Corporation	BEI promoted entrepreneurship and economic development by reducing the legal, regulatory, and administrative burden for SMEs. The project collaborated with governments to streamline legal and regulatory processes and facilitate informed and effective dialogue between the private and public sectors.	http://www.pragmacorp.com/ bei.htm
Kenya	2003-2009	**The Improved Agriculture for Smallholders Western Kenya (TASK)**	CARE International	TASK is one of five projects in the five-year Development Assistance Program (DAP) II. The primary objective of TASK was to sustainably improve food and livelihood security for 4,500 vulnerable households in Nyanza province.

In DAP I (1998- 2003), TASK's primary focus was sustainable availability of food. TASK II shifted away from training in technologies aimed at staple food production to interventions that increased commercialization of agricultural production, such as marketing and transformation of smallholder agriculture from subsistence to market oriented production. The project scaled up activities | http://pdf.usaid.gov/pdf_docs/ PDACQ778.pdf |

Country	Date	Project	Implementing & Local Partners	Description of Activities	Links
				through increased diversification of farm enterprises with improved agricultural and natural resource management skills to optimize food availability, strengthen farmer organizations, and develop markets to enhance increased returns. Participants were trained in agricultural production technologies, group organization and management, marketing, and entrepreneurship skills.	
Kyrgyz Republic	2006	**USAID Business and Economics Education Project**	Carana Corporation	The project established the Kyrgyz-American Center for Entrepreneurship Studies (KACES) at Osh Technological University. The center was the first business training school in the Kyrgyz Republic affiliated with an institution of higher education, and will improve the business environment by providing current and aspiring entrepreneurs with access to practical training and materials. It is also expected to foster greater penetration of business and entrepreneurship curriculum into higher education.	http://www.usaid.gov/locations/ europe_eurasia/press/ success/2006-07-20.html
Kyrgyz Republic	2003-2008	**Agri-Enterprise Development (KAED) Project**	International Fertilizer Development Center (IFDC)	KAED provided assistance to improve the productivity and profitability of the agricultural system. The project helped develop a trade association of private agribusinesses to deliver legal advice, technology, information, and agricultural inputs (including seeds, fertilizers, and crop protection products) to its members and to farmers. Through the Farmer-to-Farmer Program, USAID brings volunteer experts to deliver technical assistance to small and medium agribusinesses.	http://pdf.usaid.gov/pdf_docs/ PDACM077.pdf
Lebanon	2007-2009	**Lebanon Education Assistance for Development (LEAD) Program**	CHF *INJAZ Lebanon, the Rene Moawad Foundation and Union of Arab ICT Associations. Close collaboration with the Ministry of Education and Higher Education*	The LEAD program supported the quality of education in Lebanese public schools by focusing on improving the physical and psychosocial environment. The program was designed to create a healthy and safe educational environment, increase the interdependence of schools and communities, and enhance student growth outside the classroom. Local partner INJAZ Lebanon worked within the project to raise social awareness and provide extracurricular opportunities related to business and entrepreneurship. LEAD was funded under two cooperative agreements with International Orthodox Christian Charities, Incorporated, and Cooperative Housing Foundation International.	http://www.rmf.org.lb/ economy/war_relief/lead.html http://www.chfinternational. org/node/28886

106

Country	Date	Project	Implementing & Local/Partners	Description of Activities	Links
				LEAD achieved its intended results and had a significant impact in improving the learning environment in 283 Lebanese public schools during 2007 and 2008. This impact was due to the education program 1) covering 283 or 20 percent of Lebanon's 1,405 public schools in six governorates; and 2) focusing program efforts on schools with the most needs, at the request of the Government of the Republic of Lebanon. Of these 283 schools, 110 were used to shelter internally displaced persons during conflicts. The program's substantial accomplishments included the repair and/or rehabilitation of 134 public school infrastructures, provision of laboratory equipment to 104 public schools, and the facilitation of 628 medical and mental health, nutrition, drug, and social awareness sessions. In addition, 195 school clubs and 61 parent teacher associations were formed over the course of the implementation period.	
Lebanon	2008-2011	Lebanon Business Linkages Initiative	Academy for Educational Development (AED)	By targeting market driver firms in agribusiness, tourism and information and communication technology, LBLI builds on previous investments to foster sustainable growth and poverty reduction in rural Lebanon.	http://www.acdivoca.org/acdivoca/PortalHub.nsf/ID/lebanonLBLI
Liberia	2004-2010	Liberia Community Infrastructure Program	Development Alternatives, Inc. (DAI)	LCIP Phase I started in 2004 to promote quick impact community-level economic and social reintegration along with rehabilitation of community infrastructure in the aftermath of the war that ended in 2003. LCIP Phase II evolved in response to the country's transition from dependence on relief and emergency assistance to a posture of rebuilding for development. LCIP-managed programs include a Rural Apprenticeship Program (RAP), and a Private Sector Internship Program (PIP), which provides the opportunity for participants to learn a trade and business skills, gain experience by apprenticing in a business, and incubation support. After the program's completion, some apprentices are hired by the participating enterprises; others find employment elsewhere or start their own businesses. Since 2005, more than 221 businesses and 2,748 apprentices have benefited from the program nationwide.	http://liberia.usaid.gov/node/45 http://www.dai.com/work/project_detail.php?pid=29

Country	Date	Project	Implementing & Local Partners	Description of Activities	Links
MENA	2002+	The Middle East Partnership Initiative (MEPI) Middle East Entrepreneur Training Program (MEET)		MEET is specifically designed to provide skills training, professional networking, and alumni support systems to increase the managerial and entrepreneurial skills available to businesses and civil servants. Since 2002, more than 250 of the MENA region's high-potential business and civil society leaders have completed the intensive MEET training program and continue to develop skills and collaborate with other graduates via the MEET Alumni Network.	http://www.abudhabi.mepi. state.gov/index.html
Middle East: Bahrain, Jordan, Kuwait, Oman, Qatar, UAE	2008-2011	Empowering Municipalities through Local Economic Development, Relief International (EMLED)	Relief International	The EMLED or "Al Baladiyat" project supports the empowerment of municipalities, establishment of collaboration between communities, promotion of public-private partnerships, and increased sustainability for local economic development. EMLED uses innovative training techniques to increase the capacity of 575 municipal officials in 115 municipalities, representing eight municipality clusters, to engage and lead local projects through capacity building and training services on strategic planning, project design, and local economic development issues.	http://www.ri.org/story. php?ID=38
Moldova	2010-2014	Competitiveness Enhancement and Enterprise Development II (CEED II)	Chemonics International Inc.	The first phase of the CEED project bolstered the competitiveness of Moldovan private sector enterprises in the textiles and apparel, information technology, and winemaking industries. CEED II builds upon past experience to further support Moldovan enterprises' ability to successfully compete in the global marketplace. The project continues to work in the same industries and will expand activities to three others while continually focusing on the long-term goals of self-sufficiency and sustainability.	http://www.chemonics.com/ Projects/submit_search contracts.aspx?showBack =1&selPractice=%7BE55 2FD52-30C8-4628-B9DB-61794AF461AD%7D
Mongolia	2002- 2009	Growing Entrepreneurship Rapidly (GER)	CHF International	The GER Initiative endeavored to raise the quality of life for residents in Mongolia's peri-urban areas by supporting local entrepreneurship and facilitating employment opportunities for thousands of residents. The Initiative operated twenty business and employment centers, serving clients in small manufacturing (e.g., wood, metal-working, textiles), construction, agribusiness and trade services. Specific	http://www.chfinternational. org/node/27983 http://mongolia.usaid.gov/ our-work/program-archives/ ger-intitiative/

Country	Date	Project	Implementing & Local Partners	Description of Activities	Links
				services provided by the centers included: group development, consulting and training, loan facilitation, employment matching, business-to-business input and sales linkages, and business, market and legal information. During the implementation period, the GER Initiative helped create 98 new enterprises and strengthened 474 businesses, generating 522 jobs. The project partnered with 56 larger businesses to created employment and business linkages, and collaborated with key banks to provide lower-interest business loans worth over $1.9M. The initiative also matched 2,339 peri-urban residents to long-term job opportunities, and coordinated vocational training for 336 peri-urban residents.	
Morocco	2010+	**Business Innovation Center (BIC)**	Weidemann Associates, Inc.	The Business Innovation Center initiative emerged in 2010 out of discussions between major Moroccan stakeholders and USAID regarding boosting innovation in the economy and particularly regarding SMEs. The concept of a Moroccan Business Innovation Center Project Alliance (BICPA) is a collaborative sustainable replicable model to stimulate the development and success of technology SMEs and start-ups, initially in the economic capital - the Casablanca region. The thesis behind the BIC concept was that there is a need to create an effective, and, above all, sustainable and useful relative to private sector Small and Medium Enterprises' (SME) and entrepreneurs' needs. The BIC program thesis was to support the fostering of start-up and growth of technology companies in Morocco and assist emerging technology companies by providing incubation, high technology business start-up, technology commercialization, business practice and other support programs, as well as flexible space to those who need it. At present, there is a clear need to develop a consensus among the potential parties foreseen, given the emergence of important divergences of opinion or vision, and the Moroccan government's emphasis on its own Innovation plan as a cornerstone.	

Country	Date	Project	Implementing & Local Partners	Description of Activities	Links
Morocco	2005-2009	Integrated Agriculture and Agribusiness Program (AAI)	Chemonics International Inc.	AAI was a five-year program to help private enterprises and associations become more competitive through better processes, quality control, and management and marketing.	http://www.aai.ma/
Morocco	2005-2009	New Business Opportunity Program	Nathan Associates	The program helped Moroccan firms in selected sectors (Textiles/ Apparel, Leather Goods and Automotive Parts) to enter or expand their sales in the U.S. market, taking advantage of the benefits of the Free Trade Agreement.	http://www.nathaninc.com/ projects-and-cases/ morocco-new-business-opportunities-2005-2009
Pakistan	2004-2008	Advancing Learning and Employability for a Better Future (ALEF)	Academy for Educational Development (AED)	ALEF worked with agricultural training centers to prepare technicians for employment in the agribusiness sector, and directly with the private sector to increase the number of qualified young people to work in the growing tourism industry. ICT and entrepreneurial skills were integrated into all elements of the various program activities.	http://cge.aed.org/Projects/ NAfrica/c_morocco_alef.cfm
Pakistan	2009-2014	Empowering Pakistan: Entrepreneurs (EPE)	Ministry of Industries, Aik Hunar Aik Nagar (AHAN)	EPE expands market opportunities for micro and small entrepreneurs. According to projections, more than 120,000 entrepreneurs will be impacted by program activities, 75% of which will be women.	http://www.usaid.gov/pk/ sectors/growth/epe.html
Pakistan	2009-2014	Empowering Pakistan: Jobs	CARE International	The goal of the Empowering Pakistan: Jobs Project is to improve Pakistan's enabling environment for increased, equitable economic growth by strengthening its urban workforce development systems through increased access to training, jobs, and business opportunities. Activities are private-sector-led, focused on strengthening private training institutes and NGOs to meet industrial labor needs. The Project aims to improve the productivity of Pakistani firms by encouraging investment in human capital development and by opening workplaces more equitably to female workers. Public/ private partnerships are pursued to ensure scale and sustainability of workforce and micro enterprise development systems.	http://www.care.org/ careswork/projects/PAK010. asp http://www.usaid.gov/pk/ sectors/growth/epi.html

Country	Date	Project	Implementing & Local Partners	Description of Activities	Links
Pakistan	2009-2013	**Empowering Pakistan: Firms**	Chemonics International, Inc.	The USAID Pakistan Firms project will develop a dynamic, internationally competitive, business sector in Pakistan that is increasing exports, employing more people and producing higher value added products and services. The project will accomplish this by working at the policy level, with business sectors and with individual firms to improve productivity and competitiveness with a focus on 20 of Pakistan's fastest growing Districts.	http://www.usaid.gov/pk/sectors/growth/epf.html
Pakistan	2009- 2014	**Empowering Pakistan: Trade (EPT)**	*Trade Development Authority of Pakistan (TDAP), Board of Investments, Ministry of Commerce*	EPT is designed to improve the trade environment in Pakistan, resulting in expanded exports, more competitive enterprises, and increased employment opportunities. The project accomplishes this through policy level interventions, capacity building, support to duty free zones and firms in these zones engaged in export.	http://www.usaid.gov/pk/sectors/growth/ept.html
Pakistan	2006	**Pakistani Center for Entrepreneurial Excellence at the Institute for Business Administration**	J.E. Austin Associates Inc. (JEA)	In 2006, USAID funded a feasibility study for the creation of a Center for Entrepreneurial Excellence at the Institute of Business Administration (IBA) in Karachi. The assessment generated a positive response from both IBA and the Karachi private sector, and the study became a catalyst for the center's eventual creation.	http://www.usaid.gov/pk/ecgrowth/index.htm http://pdf.usaid.gov/pdf_docs/PNADI564.pdf
Paraguay	2007-2010	**Vende II**	Chemonics International Inc.	Building off of Vende I (2003- 2007) Vende II utilized the "value chain" concept to link agricultural producers, produce buyers, processing firms, and consumers, domestic and foreign. The project identified promising enterprises in three geographic areas, providing assistance to develop work plans and relieve key constraints to growth of the firm, before ending the technical assistance once the key goals were achieved, or in some cases, when it became clear that the firm was unable or unwilling to undertake key actions. Sales and exports connected to the project were more than twice the original target, exceeded the revised targets of $94 million in sales and $64 million in exports. The project's work in sesame (one of three targeted sectors which also included processed meat and	http://pdf.usaid.gov/pdf_docs/PDACR563.pdf

111

Country	Date	Project	Implementing & Local Partners	Description of Activities	Links
				textiles) helped create a new major export sector, with exports rising from less than $5 million in 2003 to more than $100 million in 2008. An estimated 10,000 farmers were connected to project activities, mostly through assistance in using improved seeds and agricultural practices.	
Swaziland	2006-2011	Swaziland Enterprise and Entrepreneurship Program (SWEEP)	TechnoServe	SWEEP's business advisors support individual entrepreneurs and their businesses throughout each stage of their development – from idea to expansion. SWEEP works with Swaziland's financial institutions to help close the gaps between their respective products and SME clients. The program also seeks to build sustainable local capacity – such as local business service providers and associations – to support entrepreneurs and SMEs and remove constraints to SME development.	http://www.technoserve.org/work-impact/locations/swaziland.html#moreabout http://swaziland.usembassy.gov/swaziland_enterprise_and_entrepreneurship_program_sweep.html
Tajikistan	2005	Policies and Opportunities for Women Entrepreneurs Readiness (POWER)	CHF International	The POWER program facilitated entrepreneurship among women by introducing policy reforms, conducting outreach and advocacy, building local capacity, holding design and business trainings, and providing much-needed networking opportunities.	http://www.chfinternational.org/node/21283
Tajikistan	2004-2006	Alternatives to Conflict in Tajikistan (ACT) program	CHF International	ACT provided Tajik youths with newfound employment opportunities and tangible alternatives to conflict, and established an Economic Opportunity Center (EOC) in the city of Isfara.	http://www.chfinternational.org/node/20965
Thailand	2002-2005	Thailand Competitiveness Initiative (TCI)	J.E. Austin Associates (JEA)	As part of its Accelerating Economic Recovery in Asia (AERA) Program, TCI was designed to develop the competitiveness of a wide variety of industry clusters in Thailand.	http://pdf.usaid.gov/pdf_docs/PDACG139.pdf

Country	Date	Project	Implementing & Local Partners	Description of Activities	Links
Turkey	2005-2006	**Turkey–U.S. Business Partnering Alliance Activity**	Carana Corporation	The project prepared a series of market perception reports, based on surveys with leading firms and business associations in five sectors—automotive, software development, marble, furniture, and lighting—along with intelligence from international players doing business in Turkey.	http://mail.caman.org/index.php?option=com_content&view=article&id=382&Itemid=61
Turkmenistan	2006-2009	**Agricultural Improvement Project**	Winrock International	The project undertook activities to build competitiveness and strengthen value chains for domestic, regional, and international markets, as well as increase rural incomes by helping farmers and agribusinesses to link with agricultural markets, produce better products and deliver consistent quality goods to local and regional markets.	http://www.winrock.org/programs/country.asp?countryid=1426#
Turkmenistan	2009+	**Private Sector Productivity**	Junior Achievement (JA)	To help young people successfully enter a market economy as employers or entrepreneurs, the program supports development of practical skills in business and economics education at the secondary school level through student-oriented activities, contests and alumni networking. The program also improves the institutional capacity of JA's operations in Turkmenistan through organizational development, strengthening partnerships with the private sector to increase sustainability and engagement with the public sector to incorporate business and economics education into the mainstream curriculum.	http://centralasia.usaid.gov/page.php?page=article-175
Turkmenistan		**Economic Reform to Enhance Competitiveness project (EREC)**	BearingPoint	The Economic Reforms to Enhance Competitiveness project provided assistance to strengthen Turkmenistan's fiscal management and create the foundation for a competitive private sector and to increased investment.	http://erecproject.net/index.php

113

Country	Date	Project	Implementing & Local Partners	Description of Activities	Links
Ukraine	2009-2012	Local Investment and National Competitiveness (LINC)	Chemonics International Inc.	LINC enhances competitiveness in Ukraine, especially in the Crimea, by using municipal and regional economic strategic planning to drive local investment and increase national competitiveness. The project supports improvement of the business-enabling environment at the national and sub-national level by promoting economic reforms, assisting localities to reduce administrative and regulatory barriers to investment, and fostering public-private partnerships. The project also is also enhancing the competitiveness of private enterprises by working with select industries, encouraging the adoption of international standards, and facilitating the movement of goods across its borders. The project inks local investment with national competitiveness in a way that harnesses Ukraine's human energy, talent, and financial resources to foster broad-based and sustainable economic growth.	http://www.chemonics.com/Projects/submit_search_contracts.aspx?showBack=1&selPractice=%7BE55 2FD52-30C8-4628-B9DB-61794AF461AD%7D
Uzbekistan	2009+	Agribusiness	Holis Konsalt	Agribusiness stimulates linkages between market-driven producers, for-profit agri-business intermediaries, and private wholesalers, processors, and retailers of agricultural products, acting as a catalyst for specific opportunities to demonstrate new ways of doing business. Assistance is provided to farms and farmer associations, intermediating agri-businesses that provide key goods and services, and buyers. In the short term, this assistance helps Uzbek private sector firms and farmers improve market-driven agricultural production; develop key market-linking agri-businesses and local capacity to understand, analyze and respond to market opportunities through marketing and market information support. In the long term, this project assists agricultural producers and processors in Uzbekistan in meeting specifications of buyers in higher income markets in terms of quality, volumes and price.	http://centralasia.usaid.gov/page.php?page=article-121&from_t=uztext
West Bank/ Gaza	2008-2011	Enterprise Development and Investment Promotion Project (EDIP)	Carana Corporation	EDIP creates partnerships with successful Palestinian businesses to accelerate business growth through access to technology, markets, and equity capital.	http://www.carana.com/index.php?option=com_content&view=article&id=390&Itemid=64

Country	Date	Project	Implementing & Local Partners	Description of Activities	Links
West Bank/ Gaza	2001-2003	Trade Facilitation Project	Chemonics International Inc.	The project worked to build capacity within the Palestinian Authority to improve transparency, security, logistics, and administrative efficiency at borders and crossings. It also assisted the private sector in the improvement of supply chain efficiency and security by building alliances between Palestinian and Israeli firms, providing advance information to crossing point managers, and introducing risk management systems.	http://www.chemonics.com/ projects/submit_search_con-tracts.aspx?showBack=1&c kCurrent=1&selPractice={E5 52FD52-30C8-4628-B9DB-61794AF461AD}
West Bank/ Gaza	2005-2009	Palestinian Agribusiness Partnership Activity (PAPA)	Carana Corporation	Through $6.1 million in cost-sharing grants, PAPA enabled seven agribusiness firms in the West Bank to expand and enhance operations to meet export standards, and opened markets for about 650 small farmers and producers of herbs, vegetables and olive oil.	http://www.carana.com/index. php?option=com_content&vie w=article&id=99&Itemid=61
West Bank/ Gaza	2004-2008	Palestine Enterprise Development (PED)	Development Alternatives, Inc. (DAI)	PED focused on strengthening democratic and market economy institutions, thereby maintaining positive momentum in the private sector and in key economic ministries so that the Palestinian economy is equipped to compete in the global market.	http://www.dai.com/work/ project_detail.php?pid=112
West Bank/ Gaza	2005- 2006	Policies and Opportunities for Women Entrepreneurs Readiness (POWER)	CHF International	POWER facilitated entrepreneurship among women by introducing policy reforms, conducting outreach and advocacy, building local capacity, holding design and business trainings, and providing much-needed networking opportunities.

The POWER pilot project exceeded all of its objectives in only half the time originally allotted to the program, directly assisting 103 women in improving their production—more than two-and-a-half times the original target of 40 women. | http://www.chfinternational. org/node/27996 |
| Yemen | 2005+ | Youth Economic Development Initiative | CHF International | The concept of the YEDI Apprenticeship Program is based on preparing the vocational labor force and providing it with the necessary labor-market skills, through both education and training, to be carried out in educational establishments (institutes) and workplaces (companies). | http://www.chfinternational .org/node/20928

http://egateg.usaidallnet.gov/ youth-economic-development-initiative |

Country	Date	Project	Implementing & Local Partners	Description of Activities	Links
Yemen	2002-2007	416(b) Program	ACDI/VOCA	The program supported broad-based agricultural and agribusiness growth in conjunction with natural resource management initiatives.	http://www.acdivoca.org/acdivoca/PortalHub.nsf/ID/westbankgazagrantsmanagement
Zambia	2005-2010	Market Access, Trade and Enabling Policies Project (MATEP)	Development Alternatives, Inc. (DAI) *ECIAfrica, Zambia Agricultural Technical Assistance Center, Ltd. (ZATAC)*	The MATEP project was a five-year USAID economic growth project designed to increase Zambia's exports of agricultural and natural resource products and tourism services into regional and international markets. The project had five closely interlinked components to achieve its export objective: Trade and Enabling Policy, Market Access, Tourism, Finance and HIV/AIDS.	http://www.dai.com/work/project_detail.php?pid=100 http://dec.usaid.gov/index.cfm?p=search.getCitation&CFID=18676629&CFTOKEN=72855350&id=s4049D26A-D566-FC5C-D2AC47A86C00F517&rec_no=166557
Zambia	2005-2010	Production, Finance and Improved Technology (PROFIT)	Development Alternatives, Inc. (DAI)	PROFIT increased smallholder client production and productivity by reducing costs of production and, together with private and public sectors, extending services to some 100,000 small farmers in high economic potential areas in Zambia. The project focused on value chains and the development of support industries, such as financial services and inputs. By 2009, 14 firms selling chemicals, fertilizer and veterinary drugs were cooperating with PROFIT to build the network for agricultural inputs and services. About 600 agents were active, serving more than 100,000 farmers and making a rapidly rising total of agent-mediated sales. Increased access to commercial agricultural products and services encouraged the evolution of smallholder practices from subsistence to emerging commercial agriculture.	http://pdf.usaid.gov/pdf_docs/PDACR843.pdf

Country	Date	Project	Implementing & Local Partners	Description of Activities	Links
Zimbabwe	2010-2015	**Zimbabwe Agricultural Competitiveness Program**	Development Alternatives, Inc. (DAI)	The Zimbabwe Agricultural Competitiveness Program is supporting the private sector-driven revitalization of Zimbabwe's agriculture economy by strengthening representative institutions, improving market infrastructure, and improving agribusiness skills, services, production, and productivity. The program relies heavily on supporting local experts and institutions, tapping into the Zimbabwean diaspora in South Africa, and incorporating local bodies directly into the planning, oversight, and monitoring of program interventions.	http://www.dai.com/work/project_detail.php?pid=256&x=8&y=8
	2004	**Diagnosing Barriers to Entrepreneurship and Assessing the Chances for Implementing Reform**	George Mason University	The publication, written at a university in the United States, offered a framework for identifying barriers to entrepreneurship and assessing the implementation potential of policies to remove barriers and channel entrepreneurship into economic development.	http://egateg.usaidallnet.gov/resources/703

117